ABORTION IN MEXICO

Engendering Latin America

ABORTION IN MEXICO

A HISTORY

NORA E. JAFFARY

UNIVERSITY OF NEBRASKA PRESS

LINCOLN

∞

Library of Congress Cataloging-in-Publication Data
Names: Jaffary, Nora E., 1968– author.
Title: Abortion in Mexico: a history / Nora E. Jaffary.
Other titles: Historia del aborto en México. English
Description: Lincoln: University of Nebraska Press,
[2024] | Series: Engendering Latin America | Includes
bibliographical references and index.
Identifiers: LCCN 2023056324
ISBN 9781496239624 (hardback)
ISBN 9781496240217 (paperback)
ISBN 9781496240613 (epub)
ISBN 9781496240620 (pdf)
Subjects: LCSH: Abortion—Mexico—History. | BISAC:
SOCIAL SCIENCE / Abortion & Birth Control | SOCIAL
SCIENCE / Women's Studies
Classification: LCC HQ767.5.M6 J344 2024 | DDC
362.1988/800972—dc23/eng/20240430
LC record available at https://lccn.loc.gov/2023056324

Designed and set in Arno Pro by Lacey Losh.

CONTENTS

TABLES

ACKNOWLEDGMENTS

Several individuals and organizations helped me produce this book. My thanks to Sonya Lipsett-Rivera for encouraging me to submit it to Nebraska, to both readers of the manuscript, to editor Emily Casillas for shepherding it through production, and to Emily Shelton for her copyediting. I thank my research assistants Hugo Rueda Ramírez and Benjamin Alonso Rascón for helping me track down judicial cases and newspaper articles in various Mexican repositories, and Dylan Wilkerson for his work translating Pope Pius IX's 1869 bull *Apostolicae Sedis* from Latin to English. Many scholars helped me figure out detailed issues and broad concepts while I was writing. They include Ed Osowski, who read the entire manuscript and provided key feedback at a crucial moment, bless him; my Concordia colleagues Bradley Craig, Shannon McSheffrey, Elena Razlogova, and Eric Reiter, who workshopped a chapter with me; and the members of the Latin American Research Group based at York University who gave me feedback on the book proposal. Thanks also to Caroline Beer, Sandra Gonzáles-Santos, and Elizabeth O'Brien for their aid with particular queries, and also to Joan Bristol, Margo Echenberg, and Jane Nicholas for friendship, inspiration, and expertise from related fields. Cassia Roth, Elizabeth O'Brien, and Jethro Hernández Berrones shared enthusiasm for the topics and stories treated here as we together produced a selection of primary sources treating reproductive history in Latin America, freely available to all at Julia Rodríguez's History of Science in Latin America and the Caribbean website (https:// mypages.unh.edu/hoslac/book/advanced-topic-reproductive-histories). The Social Sciences and Humanities Council of Canada and the John Carter Brown Library provided financial support. The interlibrary loan office at Concordia

University was also an indispensable resource. I was also aided by assistance with materials from the University of Arizona, Special Collections, and the Universidad Complutense in Madrid. As always, I am grateful for the love, humor, and engagement of my closest family members: Ed, Luc, and Simon.

This text is a slightly modified version of *Historia del aborto en México*, published in 2023 with Tirant lo Blanch in Mexico, and I thank Pablo Mijangos y González for inviting me to contribute the work for publication with Tirant. This English version includes some slight modifications: a longer discussion is included here of material treating the ancient discourse of abortion's prohibition, drawn from a paper I presented at the 2022 Congreso de Mexicanistas, as are some twentieth-century newspaper articles collected in the summer of 2023 from the Hemeroteca Nacional in Mexico City. There are also a small number of additional scholarly works included in this version not discussed in the Spanish version, along with some more contextual information about the development of both Mexico's independence revolution and the 1910 Revolution, both of which I judged unnecessary for a Mexican readership. Because this work is based on a topic about which I have previously published, I have drawn from many of the same primary sources used in earlier publications to write chapter 1, which treats the period from early postconquest history to 1870. In its current form, this discussion benefits from more developed analysis and the enlarged contextual framework possible with the comprehensive consideration of all previously used sources.

ABBREVIATIONS

AC   Acción Católica (Catholic Action)

AGN   Archivo General de la Nación (General Archive of the Nation)

CMF   Coalición de Mujeres Feministas (Coalition of Feminist Women)

GIEA   Grupo Interdisciplinario para el Estudio de Aborto en México (Interdisciplinary Group for the Study of Abortion in Mexico)

GIRE   Grupo de Información en Reproducción Elegida (Reproductive Choice Educational Collective)

IACHR   Inter-American Commission on Human Rights

IVF   in vitro fertilization

MNM   Movimiento Nacional de Mujeres (National Movement of Women)

NOM   Norma Oficial Mexicana (Mexican Official Norm)

PAN   Partido de Acción Nacional (Party of National Action)

PDM   Partido Demócrata Mexicano (Mexican Democratic Party)

PRD   Partido de Revolución Democrático (Revolutionary Democratic Party)

PRI   Partido Revolucionario Institucional (Institutional Revolutionary Party)

SCJN Suprema Corte de Justicia de la Nación
      (National Supreme Court of Justice)
TSJDF Tribunal Superior de Justicia del Distrito Federal
      (Superior Tribunal of the Federal District)
UNAM Universidad Nacional Autónoma de México
      (National Autonomous University of Mexico)

ABORTION IN MEXICO

INTRODUCTION

All of our families harbor stories of unplanned, impossible pregnancies. Some of the women in my own family, willingly or unwillingly, carried such pregnancies to term. Some, lawfully or unlawfully, aborted their pregnancies. The same is surely true for you. Across time and space, these women's stories yield many parallels. This book places the experiences of such women, their communities, and the legal contexts in which they lived in historical perspective through its discussion of the history of abortion in Mexico from the colonial period to the present. It examines Catholic attitudes toward abortion, the medical practices used over time to interrupt pregnancy, and the relationship between these attitudes and practices and changing constructions of gender. The book's central focus, however, is on the evolving regulation of abortion in the law. This is a long history to pack into a short book. Let me introduce it by telling you some of the central things I have uncovered in my research on this important and divisive topic.

Abortion in Mexico: The Present and the Past

At the time of writing, Mexico is at a pivotal moment in terms of its judicial and legislative apprehension of abortion. In line with many parts of Western Europe and the Americas (with the significant exception of the United States) for the past twenty years, Mexico has moved to liberalize abortion law. Mexico City initiated a series of legislative changes to what was then called the Distrito Federal's (Federal District's) abortion laws in 2000 with a set of modifications to the capital's penal code, which had endured largely unchanged since 1931. These reforms are referred to as Ley Robles (the Robles law), after feminist

Rosario Robles, Mexico City's Partido de Revolución Democrático (Revolutionary Democratic Party, or PRD) mayor, who initiated the modifications. The Robles law involved several changes to the 1931 code. Among others it deemed that no sanctions for abortion would apply when pregnancy threatened a woman's health (rather than only her life), when severe genetic or congenital conditions threatened the survival of the "product of conception," or when a woman was impregnated in instances of nonconsensual artificial insemination.[1] Further, it eliminated those clauses that allowed lighter sentencing in what are known as the *honoris causa* qualifications on abortion sentencing. These clauses, incorporated into the Distrito Federal's 1871 penal code, had allowed for lighter sentencing of women convicted of abortion who were not of ill repute, those who had successfully concealed their pregnancies, and those who had conceived outside of marriage.

The 2000 reforms emerged from a complex context. The forces that helped establish it included two decades of feminist demands for increased reproductive rights and the international acknowledgment of the imperative of expanding such rights expressed in two United Nations conferences in 1994 (Cairo) and 1995 (Beijing), both of which addressed internationally high rates of female mortality due to unsafe abortions. The 2000 reforms also arrived in the wake of the historic presidential elections of the same year, in which the Partido Revolucionario Institucional (Institutional Revolutionary Party, or PRI) lost power after eight decades of monopoly of the office, an event presaged by its loss of the mayorship of Mexico City to the PRD under the leadership of Robles's predecessor, Cuauhtémoc Cárdenas, in 1997. Opponents of the Robles law challenged its legality before the national Supreme Court, the Suprema Corte de Justicia de la Nación (SCJN), but in 2002 the court upheld the constitutionality of the law. However, the court did not base its judgment on assessments of either women's constitutional rights to bodily autonomy or on a negation of the idea of fetal personhood. Rather, it based its position on a technicality: that the legal changes the Robles law introduced did not challenge either the criminality of abortion or the notion of fetal personhood, but only conservatively dictated that abortion would remain criminal but would not be sanctioned—that is, punished.[2]

Further dramatic legal changes occurred in 2007, when Mexico City again revised its penal code to legalize abortion during the first trimester of pregnancy, joining only two other Latin American countries where the procedure was lawful at the time.[3] A PRI deputy, Armando Tonatiuh González, introduced the act, which he justified in terms of the constitutionality of the separation of church and state, the argument that first-trimester human embryos were not "people," and the assertion that the penalization of abortion curtailed women's human and civil rights. Among its key elements was the 2007 law's definition of pregnancy as "the period of time in the process of human reproduction that begins with the implementation of the embryo in the endometria."[4] The law did not classify the termination of the product of conception before this date as an abortion and, therefore, did not penalize it. The 2007 changes also mandated that abortion would be available free of charge in public hospitals in Mexico City, and available at moderate prices for women from other states or countries. The SCJN heard legal challenges to the 2007 law the following year and again upheld it, this time on a more substantive ruling, as judicial scholar Alejandro Madrazo observes. It asserted that "there were no constitutional grounds to claim that a fetus has a right to life" and judged that decriminalizing first-trimester abortion was an "ideal" means to safekeep women's biological autonomy and their health.[5]

The Secretaría de Salud issued an additional significant regulation affecting women's access to abortion in 2009. Norma Oficial Mexicana (NOM) 046, a mandatory regulation concerning violence against women, had broad jurisdiction over medical, public health, and social service institutions. Among other regulations NOM 046 required the provision of abortion to women and girls impregnated in instances of rape who requested the service.[6] While the Distrito Federal's 1931 penal code, and all states in Mexico following it, had decriminalized abortion in cases of rape, state agencies in the second half of the twentieth century did not always follow the law on this point. The Mexican state was forced to adopt NOM 046 in the wake of Paulina del Carmen Ramírez Jacinto's successful and instrumental suit with the Inter-American Commission on Human Rights (IACHR), settled in 2007. Ramírez Jacinto, then aged fourteen, had been raped and impregnated during a home robbery in Mexicali (Baja California) in 1999. Although Baja California's penal code permitted first-trimester abortions in such cases, various medical and legal authorities, including the state attorney general and medical staff at the Mexicali General Hospital, repeatedly and illegally blocked her access to the procedure. In the wake of her enforced pregnancy and the subsequent birth of her son, Ramírez Jacinto's representatives lodged a petition with the IACHR, which accepted their claim. The IACHR resolved the case with the Mexican state and the State of Baja California in 2007 for a cash settlement, a public acknowledgment of the state's culpability, and a governmental commitment to enforce a broad set of directives combatting violence against women and supporting women's rights to lawfully terminate pregnancies.[7]

In the fall of 2021, the SCJN issued a series of momentous judgements than even its earlier ruling upholding the Federal District's legalization of first-trimester abortion. On September 7 it issued a unanimous ruling in a case involving the state of Coahuila's penal code, which had decreed that women who voluntarily aborted, or those who enabled the abortion, should be imprisoned for one to three years.[8] The SCJN declared the Coahuila's law unconstitutional, ruling that the "product of gestation deserves protection that increases as the pregnancy advances."[9] Nevertheless it ruled that this protection did not supersede the rights of women and pregnant people to reproductive liberty. The ruling, since it applied only to Coahuila's state code, rather than constituting the last word on abortion in Mexico, will no doubt represent the beginning of another set of legal and judicial conflicts that will unfold in the coming decade as other states in the federation bring their codes in line with the ruling, which, given its unanimity in the court, sets a binding precedent for subsequent state and federal judges.[10]

Two days later the SCJN ruled against the lawfulness of state constitutions decreeing that human life began at conception, or that embryos possessed protections equal to persons, and reserved for Mexico's General Constitution the right to establish personhood. Finally, a few days after this, it issued a decision challenging a clause of the 2018 Ley General de Salud (General Law of Health), which had granted medical personnel the right to conscientiously object to the performance of particular procedures, as the court explained, "without establishing limits necessary to ensure patients' rights to health care."[11] One of the rulings' interesting international repercussions, coinciding as they did with increasingly restrictive legislation on abortion access north of the border in Texas, was that, in their wake, pro-choice organizers in northern Mexico responded immediately by organizing to assist women in Texas, a state that in May 2021 made abortions illegal in virtually all instances.[12]

Mexico, like many places, has just entered a dramatic new era of legal abortion access, following three decades of heated conflict between pro-life and pro-choice advocates. Current generations are inclined to assume that the social and ethical tensions that abortion raises today were likely the same in the past, but this is not the case. First, the practice of abortion is in our own day much more strongly condemned, at least by a portion of the population, than it was in centuries past. If denunciations for the crime of abortion can be understood to indicate its popular condemnation, it is notable that in the colonial period, when we might have expected the imperative to protect family honor would have been highest, and Catholic values have been most strongly defended, few Mexicans actively denounced abortion. Almost nobody—not regular Mexicans, not state authorities, not official representatives of the church—condemned it in the powerful terms that we might today encounter at a political rally or on a Twitter feed. Few people reported women for the crime to secular or sacred authorities, and even smaller numbers of religious or civil authorities pursued investigations against those denounced.

In our own day, national and international pro-life organizations, such as Opus Dei and ProVida, and political parties from both the Right (Partido de Acción Nacional; Party of National Action, or PAN) and the Left, represented by President Andrés Manuel López Obrador's Movimiento de Regeneración Nacional (MORENA), voice strong connections between Catholic doctrine and their anti-abortion positions. At the end of the twentieth century, political mobilization around abortion centered around such initiatives as the state legislature of Chiapas's unsuccessful 1991 attempt to support elective maternity. Catholic organizing was also imperative in mobilizing seventeen state legislatures to pass new laws asserting that human life begins at conception shortly after the Federal District's depenalization of first-trimester abortion in 2007.[13] Similarly, such groups are in part responsible for the increase in denunciations and prosecutions for abortion that have been on the rise outside of Mexico City since the capital liberalized abortion in 2007.[14] Lay Catholic political organizing has been effective, and it has been powerful. It is also worth acknowledging that it has been very recent.

Second, the recent judicial decisions relating to abortion, like much of its late twentieth- and early twenty-first-century legal and social discussion, focused particularly on the comparative evaluation of fetal rights (and value) versus pregnant persons' rights (and value). However, my examination of abortion's history in Mexico reveals how very recently such questions have become the focus of attention in assessing either the morality or legality of abortion. Until the late twentieth century, the discussion of fetal personhood and fetal rights was a marginal consideration for the law, to judges, to wider communities in Mexico, and even for the Catholic Church. Instead, for much of Mexican history, the imperative of protecting women's reputations of sexual honor was a matter of far greater import than was the question of fetal personhood. Elyse Singer similarly observes that in the twentieth and early twenty-first centuries, abortion in Mexico was primarily opposed not because of the issue of the destruction of "fetal life" but because of its challenge to women's traditional social roles due to the "threat that abortion authorizes against Catholic definitions of sacrificial femininity."[15]

Since the colonial period, and in the first decades after it, both state representatives and community members have expressed anxiety or even outrage about the loss of familial honor that pre- or extramarital pregnancy signified. Historically, elite men of Spanish descent required chastity in their spouses as a guarantee that both nobility and blood purity would be preserved in their lines of descent. Illegitimacy and race mixture were both grounds for denial of noble status, and even of more basic social advancement. Over the course of the colonial era, and in the century after it, growing numbers of non-elite populations began espousing the same views.[16] In the small community of Coixtlahuaca, Oaxaca, in 1849, for example, the godfather of an Indigenous woman, Isidora López, was so incensed that her premarital impregnation by his son threatened his family's honorable standing that he tied her to a ladder and whipped her severely. He declared that he inflicted the punishment "because she was blind to the rage she had caused him with her scandalous practices which defamed his house."[17] López's story does not seem greatly different from that of a seventeen-year-old whom sociologist Joaquina Erviti interviewed in 1997 in Morelos and who explained she had hidden her premarital pregnancy from her parents because, if they had discovered it, to save the family honor "they could have hit me or for what I had done, *forced me to marry against my will.*"[18]

Despite their appearance of enduring stability, perceptions and practices relating to sexual honor and abortion have undergone substantial change across

6

time. A majority of women prosecuted for attempting to conceal premarital pregnancies through abortion or infanticide in the late nineteenth century, for instance, acknowledged that they did so to protect their own or their family's honor or out of fear of their families punishing them for its loss. Such concerns, featured prominently in the clauses treating the crimes of abortion and infanticide in the Federal District's penal code of 1871, anachronistically preserved in several states' penal codes right up through the present moment. However, in the second half of the twentieth century, straitened personal finances, rather than the preservation of honor, became the motivation many women provided when interviewed about why they had sought abortions.[19]

Other elements of Mexico's abortion history reveal further long continuities. These include the endurance across centuries of the knowledge and consumption of plant-based medicines that could be used as effective abortifacients. Pre-Columbian medical healers possessed sophisticated knowledge of pregnancy and childbirth and used their wealth of botanical expertise to ease labor, care for parturient women, and provoke miscarriages in cases of undesired pregnancies. Knowledge of such medicines, alongside the incorporation of African and European abortifacients, persisted through the viceregal era, the nineteenth century, and, indeed, up to the present. A few years ago, Ricardo Reyes Chilpa, a chemist who researches the chemistry and pharmacology of medicinal plants at the Universidad Autónoma Nacional de México (UNAM), advised me to see if I could acquire a sample of *cihuapatli*, the aster flower, an abortifacient dating back to the pre-Columbian period used by Mexican midwives. Taking his advice I ventured to the Mercado Sonora, the sprawling "witchcraft" market located next to La Merced in downtown Mexico City. In just a few moments' wander, I located a vendor selling a large selection of dried plants who stocked cihuapatli. Asking me to step into an alcove out of the bustle of her other customers, she instructed me on how to make a tea with a small quantity of the plant to keep my menses regular, or to prepare a larger dose, should I need to provoke a miscarriage. Although her clientele, like many Mexican women, continue to use such preparations, since the mid-1980s they have increasingly relied on the ingestion of pharmaceuticals mifepristone and misoprostol to provoke medicinal abortions, echoing women's historic use of plant-based remedies like cihuapatli and *altamisa* (mugwort).

Besides medicinal abortions, this book also discusses surgical abortions, meaning procedures that involve physical intervention into the cervix or uterus, even though such procedures do not usually involve cutting, an act normally associated with surgery. Readers may assume, as I did before I began researching this history, that surgical abortions, whether legal or illegal, were a product of the mid-twentieth century. In fact they are much older. Some of the earliest Spanish chroniclers of postcontact Mexico described how pre-Columbian midwives were adept performers of embryotomies, dissecting and removing embryos that had ceased to give signs of life, from pregnant women's uteruses. As Bernardino de Sahagún recorded some time before 1577: "When the baby dies inside the mother: the midwife with a knife of obsidian stone cuts the dead body inside the mother and takes it out in pieces. In this way, they free the mother from death."[20]

Early modern and nineteenth-century obstetrical texts described how hooks or other instruments might be used to break the amniotic sac that surrounds a fetus to induce labor, including early in a pregnancy to induce an abortion, but warned midwives against such practices, with what degree of efficacy we do not know.[21] By the last decades of the nineteenth century, physicians in Mexico regularly researched and published about their performance of surgical abortions, and many prominent obstetricians and surgeons continued defending such procedures until the 1940s. Although some doctors continued to perform and advocate for the legality of performing abortions through the twentieth century, the dominant position of many professional medical associations became anti-abortionist in the early 1950s.

Organization and Sources

Abortion in Mexico puts the current state of abortion's legal status in historical perspective by examining its history in three broad time periods. Chapter 1 covers the colonial period and the first five decades after independence up until the promulgation of the Federal District's 1871 penal code that became the template for other states' criminal codes shortly thereafter. This first chapter addresses this sizable timespan because the legal foundation upon which courts assessed abortion did not change between the viceregal and immediate postindependence eras. Up until 1871, and often even after it, Mexican justices continued to refer to the same legal codes and practices, principally those decreed in the thirteenth-century legal code of Castilian king Alfonso X, *Las Siete Partidas* (The seven-part code). In theory, as justices trying cases in this era observed, the *Partidas* called for the death penalty for the crime of abortion. In practice few judges found women guilty of the crime, and their penalties were nowhere greater than terms of imprisonment of greater than six years.[22] Other continuities characterized the era treated in chapter 1. First, women continued to use the same methods of abortion induction, principally the ingestion of plant-based abortifacients, across this long period. Second, although denunciations for the crime were somewhat higher in the 1830s and 1840s in Yucatán and Puebla, many other parts of Mexico, including the capital and the states of Oaxaca, Tlaxcala, and Sonora had consistently low rates of denunciation for the crime throughout this era, suggesting that, before the last decades of the nineteenth century, neither the public nor sacred or state authorities prioritized the policing of abortion.

Chapter 2 examines abortion's history during the sixty-year period between the promulgation of the 1871 penal code and its next most significant revision in 1931. This was an era of dramatic change in abortion practice and penalization in comparison to the era that preceded it, although greater stasis occurred within this period, despite the distinction studies of Mexican history conventionally make between the Porfirian (1876–1910) and Revolutionary (1910–40) eras. In keeping with the liberalizing tendencies of the European codes that influenced it, the 1871 Federal District's penal code modernized the treatment of abortion dictated in the *Partidas,* mandating terms of imprisonment rather than corporal punishment for the crime and exempting women from punishment for abortion whose life pregnancy or childbirth endangered. The 1871 code was also of its era in terms of its view of its attempted mathematical calculation of extenuating and attenuating circumstances that should dictate the severity of sentences for those convicted, depending not on the status of the fetus but on the degree of harm to her sexual honor that an extramarital pregnancy represented to a pregnant woman. In a reflection of the priorities of such considerations among a broader set of women from across Mexico's demographic groups, this era is also marked by much higher rates of denunciation for abortion (as for infanticide) than was the case in earlier decades of the nineteenth century. The period from 1871 to 1930 also witnessed the development of surgical techniques of abortion that medical professionals studied, practiced, and defended at a time when religious discourse about the sinfulness of abortion was largely unspoken in Mexico despite papal decrees in 1869 (*Apostolicae Sedis*) and 1880 (*Arcanum Divinae*) that directly or indirectly condemned abortion.

The book's final chapter covers the period from 1931 until the end of the twentieth century, starting with the creation of the Distrito Federal's postrevolutionary penal code, which included the novel regulation that women who aborted because they had been raped should not be penalized, but in many other respects maintained much of the 1871 code, including its requirements that judges evaluate pregnant women's sexual honor in determining the severity for those convicted of the crime. In the early 1930s, both Catholic opponents of abortion and Socialist and eugenics-inspired advocates of the practice organized support for their positions, but neither side succeeded in dramatically altering the legal regulation of abortion. The states of Yucatán, Chiapas, and Chihuahua all exceptionally passed penal codes in 1938 that decriminalized abortion in cases of pregnant women's extreme poverty.

The mid-twentieth century witnessed declining rates of denunciation and prosecution for abortion, and these remained low until the successful liberalization of abortion law brought it more urgently into public focus after 2000. The mid-twentieth century was also marked by a change in the dominant position that professional medical associations adopted toward abortion. In earlier decades medical schools educated students about the performance of surgical abortions, and physicians unashamedly published articles concerning such treatments, including in the National Medical Academy's flagship journal, the *Gaceta médica de México* (Medical gazette of Mexico). However, by the early 1950s, obstetrical and surgical associations, if not all individual practitioners, in speeches and publications, chilled to the practice. They sometimes declared that their positions were inspired by Catholic doctrine, although the Mexican Catholic Church, hampered as it was by the strict secularization decreed by the country's 1917 Constitution, did not make overt interventions in the question of abortion practice until the two final decades of the twentieth century.

In this era feminist groups who had united to form the Coalición de Mujeres Feministas (Coalition of Feminist Women, or CMF) in 1976 worked as educators, activists, activists, and lobbyists on the campaign to fight for "voluntary motherhood," which along with abortion sought to increase sex education, the accessibility of contraception, and the termination of forced sterilization. Feminist groups and politicians, influenced by the federal government's reversal of its decades-old population policy, helped influence the beginnings of liberalization in state penal codes in the 1980s. However, significant changes to abortion law as well as shifts in public attitudes to the morality of abortion did not occur until the legal changes of 2000, the year that marked the beginning of a series of significant legislative and judicial victories for supporters of expanded abortion rights, who were aided by the research and educational campaigns of the Grupo de Información en Reproducción Elegida (Reproductive Choice Educational Collective, or GIRE), an organization formed in 1992.

This book focuses on abortion's legal history. Understanding changes in Mexican abortion law matters because its legality dramatically impacts the lives of individual women, their families, and medical personnel. However, changes in the law are not always accompanied by changes in practice. Abortion has not been criminal in cases of rape since the 1930s, yet widespread ignorance of this legal right, or a rejection of its validity, has meant that through the twentieth century, pregnant women did not always seek abortions in such circumstances, nor did medical personnel always facilitate them. An anti-abortion pamphlet that I picked up in a Mexico City church twenty years ago confusingly advises its readers that they should not be preoccupied with the idea that raped women should be permitted to abort because "fortunately few rapes are followed by pregnancies."[23] In a 1975 survey of 411 women in Mexico City, only 38 percent of respondents agreed abortion should be allowable in cases of rape.[24] A majority of medical students studying at one medical school in Mexico City in the early 1990s were also ignorant of the fact that the law permitted women in such circumstances to abort their pregnancies.[25] Similarly, the right of all Mexicans to be determine the number of spacing of their children became constitutional in 1974, and yet, as potent as this declaration might be if applied to decisions about individual reproductive control, it was not until 2008 that the country's Supreme Court invoked this right in issuing a judgment upholding the legality of Mexico City's 2007 decriminalization of first-trimester abortions. In some instances pregnant women or medical personnel are ignorant of the law. In other moments—for example, in the context of many state legislatures' surreptitious incremental liberalization of abortion law beginning in the late

1970s—the national state, then federally controlled by the PRI, purposefully silenced diffusion of information about changes to abortion law.

Moreover, changes in rates of criminal investigations for abortion, characterized across time by its hidden and private nature, do not necessarily reflect changes in abortion practice but may instead depict changes in social attitudes. Criminal courts in the state of Sonora, for instance, tried an increased number of women in the mid-nineteenth century for the crimes of infanticide and abortion. This was not because more women were terminating pregnancies or more frequently killing their newborns, but because, as Laura Shelton argues, the changing context of accelerated modernization prompted in their male peers "a local anxiety to make evident the upholding of public morality."[26] Conversely, during one period in which criminal prosecution for abortion seems to have been very low, in the last three decades of the twentieth century, the rates of women who aborted their pregnancies was high. One 2006 study found that before depenalization, 33 of every 1,000 women of reproductive age in Mexico terminated their pregnancies.[27] Ministry of Health statistics from 2009 recorded that 1,025,669 women were discharged from hospitals after being treated for medical complications resulting from induced abortions.[28] Enormous discrepancies have existed at different moments between law and practice, and even more important than law for understanding the dimensions of abortion's enactment and censure in modern Mexico is the apprehension of the amorphous state of public attitudes to abortion, which affected individuals who might feel justified in pursuing (or prohibiting) abortions and medical personnel who might condone or condemn their provision.

I construct the history of abortion in Mexico from the point of view of a social, cultural, and legal historian of colonial and nineteenth-century Mexico. I have worked, for the past fifteen years, with criminal trials from various archives in Mexico City, Oaxaca, Puebla, Tlaxcala, and Mérida. My knowledge of these cases, the laws addressed in them, and the women and men who populated them forms the foundation of this book. It is also my familiarity with this older history that allowed me to appreciate the novelty of late twentieth-century attitudes toward abortion. I have reconstructed medical perspectives by drawing from literature of various kinds: textbooks, theses, lectures, and published articles. I have apprehended Catholic perspectives by looking at papal decrees and ecclesiastical responses to these from within Mexico as well as the publications of lay Catholic organizations.

A brief word of explanation about terms may be useful here. The Spanish term *aborto* has two quite different meanings in Mexico. The English word "abortion" always refers to the intentional termination of a pregnancy while "miscarriage" connotes an unintentional, accidental termination. But the same term, *aborto*, can refer to both situations in Spanish, provoking some confusion, particularly in historical contexts. Most often this book uses "involuntary abortion" or "misbirth" to refer to situations that in English would be called "miscarriages." Spanish sources also use the term *criatura* to refer to what English sources might separately term a "fetus," a "newborn," and an "infant." The word would translate improperly as "creature" because in English this term implies a strangeness or inhumanity that it does not imply in Spanish. For this reason I have normally left *criatura* in the original Spanish in the text rather than trying to translate it. Readers should also be aware that, throughout the text, I have left spelling and accenting in the original forms found in historical documents; these sometimes differ from current usage. Lastly, a geographical note: even though the Mexican capital became officially known as La Ciudad de México (Mexico City) in 2016, this book most often refers to the capital, and particularly its penal codes, as the Distrito Federal (Federal District), because this was how it was labeled at the time the state enacted most of the codes discussed. That suffices for caveats and qualifications. Here we go into the history.

1

1519–1870

In the town of San Antonio Jacala (in present-day Hidalgo) in 1786, a fifteen-year-old girl of Spanish descent launched a lawsuit in ecclesiastical court against her second cousin for breach of promise to marry. In the course of her testimony, Juana Trinidad Márquez revealed that her cousin had impregnated her after vowing he would marry her and then, upon learning of her pregnancy, had counseled her to ingest herbs to provoke a miscarriage. Márquez confessed she had taken altamisa (mugwort) and miscarried "an animated fetus." The ecclesiastical judge who heard the case sentenced Márquez to a period of supervised confession, communion, and prayer and six months' *depósito* (supervised reclusion in a respectable house) and required her cousin to perform the same spiritual penance, as well as one year of exile from his home parish. In addition, he had to pay a fine of one hundred pesos to Márquez.[1]

Several elements of this early lawsuit are representative of abortion's history in the viceregal era, which also typify its development in the first five decades after independence. First, Márquez, like most women in preconquest, viceregal, and nineteenth-century Mexico, had access to and knowledge of plant-based medicines in use for hundreds of years on both sides of the Atlantic to control fertility by provoking miscarriages. Second, despite the existence of both sacred and secular prohibitions on abortion, it is telling that Márquez's admission that she had aborted an animated fetus did not overly trouble either the defendant herself or the court who tried the case. If she had considered abortion morally inexcusable, she would not have initiated the lawsuit or confessed to the act. Although her judge did refer to the "terrible sin of abortion" in his sentence, the court focused its investigation on determining whether

Márquez had been seduced by the promise of marriage and on establishing the degree of blood relations between Márquez and her cousin. The court pursued no questions about how she had acquired altamisa or how she had known it would work, and all of the witnesses examined testified about the couple's relationship to one another; no further discussion of the abortion consumed the court's attention.

The final element of this case that speaks to the broader history of abortion in viceregal and nineteenth-century Mexico is its rarity. People often assume that Mexicans would have more stridently opposed abortion in the period before the country formally moved toward secularization, when Catholicism had greater political and social power than it does now. Not so. Márquez's case was one of only four cases for the crime of abortion that I have located that were prosecuted in criminal or religious courts in the viceregal period. The combined holdings of over eight judicial archives in several Mexican states in the nineteenth century turned up only ten other cases of abortion tried in five decades after Mexican independence. Taking the absence of abortion's prosecution as a starting place, this chapter details the legal prohibitions on abortion that existed in viceregal and postindependence Mexico, lays out the evidence for the paucity of abortion cases that the public denounced and that authorities prosecuted in the colonial era and in the first three quarters of the nineteenth century, and offers some explanations for this lacuna.[2]

This chapter shows that the most central aspects of heated present-day discussions of abortion were alien to the colonial and nineteenth-century past. Unlike now, rarely in this earlier period did anyone discuss abortion as the taking of a human life, a life created at the moment of conception. On the rare occasions prior to the 1870s that Mexicans expressed abhorrence over abortion, they did so because they feared that the act deprived the fetus of access to baptism, a rite that would ensure the salvation of the human soul. Contemporaries believed that if baptism occurred before death, then the outcome for a fetus who died at birth was still a happy one. Another difference from our day involves public attitudes to policing reproduction. The small numbers of community members who denounced women to courts for committing abortion in this earlier era stands in stark contrast to the increase in such denunciations beginning in the late nineteenth century. Unlike in later periods, members of the public appear to have believed that scrutinizing individual women's reproductive decisions was neither their right nor their responsibility.

Although this chapter focuses on abortion history, it also discusses the history of infanticide as well. Although Mexicans normally viewed the acts as distinctive, both medical and legal experts and members of the public occasionally used the terms interchangeably. In Benita Mex's 1858 trial, originating in Izamal, Yucatán, the defendant was charged with infanticide even though her crime, rather than murdering a newborn, lay in throwing herself out of a tree while pregnant, allegedly in order to produce a miscarriage.[3] In other cases judges and witnesses moved back and forth between the two terms as though not making a distinction between the death of a fetus and that of a newborn. For example, María Luciana, tried in 1861 by the Tribunal Superior del Distrito Federal (TSJDF), is described on the title page of her dossier as investigated "under suspicion of being the agent of her abortion," but on the first page summarizing her case, her dossier indicates that the court has taken first steps to investigate her "for suspicion of infanticide."[4] Along with the fact of the blended perception of these crimes, I also draw on evidence from infanticide as well as abortion trials because many more of the former exist than do the latter, so details from these cases provide a useful supplement to evidence in abortion trials.[5]

Catholic Doctrine to 1869

Given the current-day primacy within the Christian church of the position that life begins at conception, it is remarkable how ambiguous the church's position on this question was in the early modern period, and how little attention the church paid to abortion in Mexico during the colonial era, even though today pro-life activists in Mexico and beyond claim that the Catholic Church has always opposed abortion and has always identified human life as beginning at the moment of conception.[6] Pro-life supporters trace the genealogical origins of unchanging Catholic opposition to abortion through the following intellectual genealogy: Aristotle, Augustine, Aquinas, and a series of early modern and modern popes—Sixtus V, Innocent XI, Pius IX, Pius XI, and John Paul II.[7] Pro-life activists present these authors as forming a coherent and consistent intellectual foundation supporting the idea of fetal personhood. In reality, however, their ideas on abortion were often eclectic, contradictory, and ambiguous.

Aristotle discusses abortion in various works. In *Generation of Animals*, he devotes a great deal of attention to determining whether and when male and female embryos acquire rational souls. Pinpointing his conclusion is a challenge, but he does indicate that male embryos have a stronger claim to a rational soul than females because the essence of male embryos is semen, and "it is plain ... that semen both has soul, and is soul, potentially."[8] (The female, unfortunately for her, remained, "as it were, a mutilated male.")[9]

The central observation that subsequent writers attributed to Aristotle is the notion that male embryos acquire a soul at forty days, and females at eighty. As far as I have determined, Aristotle discusses this temporal distinction in only one passage in *The History of Animals*. There he writes: "In the case of male children the first movement usually occurs on the right-hand side of the womb and about the fortieth day, but if the child be a female then on the left-hand side about the ninetieth day."[10] Basing his observations on tiny miscarried embryos that he placed in water and studied, he also notes that if a male embryo aborted at the fortieth day were placed in water, it held together "in a sort of membrane," and that the embryo itself, "as large as the large kind of ants," was fully formed, with limbs, a penis, and eyes, "but the female embryo, if it suffer abortion in the first three months, is as a rule found to be undifferentiated."[11] In this passage Aristotle refers to both "quickening" and what he called "formation" and distinguished them from his detailed discussion of the acquisition of a rational soul. Later writers, beginning with Augustine and continuing with Aquinas, folded the two discussions together. Aquinas claims to echo Aristotle's position on abortion and the soul, asserting that "human life starts only with the infusion of the rational soul into the fetal body around forty days after conception."[12]

One final point about Aristotle: although the pro-life movement has claimed Aristotle for their origin story, his writings on the subject are sometimes contradictory. In *Politics*, for instance, he comments, "Let there be a law that no *deformed* child shall live," and that "when couples have children in excess, let abortion be procured before sense and life have begun; what may or may not be lawfully done in these cases depends on the question of life and sensation."[13]

Throughout the medieval era, Christian theologians and canonists had debated the question of the circumstances under which abortion should be considered immoral or criminal. Gratian's twelfth-century canon *Aliquando* specified that no soul existed "before the form," indicating that abortion was homicide only after fetal "formation." The question remained unsettled through the high Middle Ages as to when fetal "vivification" or "ensoulment" occurred, with some writers following the fourteenth-century John of Naples, who posited that abortion before "ensoulment" was justified to preserve the life of the mother, while others believed that abortion was a sin at any moment after conception.

The papacy produced a strong condemnation of abortion in Pope Sixtus V's bull *Effraenatum*, meaning "without restraint" (1588), a directive formulated in response to his perception of rampant prostitution in Rome that established excommunication as punishment for those who procured or assisted abortions and reserved the power of absolution for such crimes exclusively to the Holy See.[14] In response Italian bishops and vicars petitioned the Congregation of Bishops to modify the bull on behalf of women who had ingested abortifacients to prevent social dishonor and of physicians who had aided them, none of whom were able to travel to Rome to plead for absolution.[15] In 1591 Sixtus's second successor, Gregory XIV, issued the *Sedes Apostolicae*, a modification of the earlier bull in which he specified that excommunication for abortion applied only to animated fetuses, which, following Aquinas, he dated to forty days for males and eighty for females. *Sedes Apostolicae* also returned to confessors the right to absolve penitents from the crime of aborting nonanimated fetuses.[16]

Like their Italian counterparts, Mexican clerics resisted the notion that the papacy alone should control absolution for abortion, although, in Mexico, the church hierarchy did not think the power should remain exclusively in the hands of individual confessors. Among the many regulations that the council of Mexican clerics published at its third Provincial Council meeting in 1585 (three years in advance of Sixtus's bull) was an articulation of clerical responsibilities and jurisdictions. The Mexican council listed a set of "terrible and grave crimes and sins" over which bishops on their own authority possessed the power to absolve excommunicated subjects, but only with special license from archbishops. At the top of the list was "voluntary homicide or procured and executed abortions."[17] In the eighteenth century, the diocese of Mexico updated its discussion of those sins that should be reserved for absolution by bishops. Citing both Sixtus V's and Gregory XIV's decrees, the diocese noted that its bishops reserved the right to absolve cases of abortions of nonanimated fetuses but remarked that no special dispensation was required in cases of abortions that had merely been attempted but not executed. In such instances individual confessors could dispense abortion.[18]

The text commented, in addition, on other instances in which confessors could claim the right to absolve abortions: "Neither does this reservation apply to those who takes or gives medicine to cure an illness without which the mother would die even though an abortion might indirectly follow from it, since the fetus is not animated, given that the male is animated at thirty or forty days and the female at fifty or eighty."[19] In 1816 fray José Ximeno revised the question and commented in his text *Opúsculo sobre los catorce casos reservados* (Treatise on the fourteen reserved cases), indicating those whose absolution was reserved for bishops alone, that "immediately after copulation, it can not be said correctly that there is a fetus, but only that one exists once the seeds are united and fertilized with maternal warmth, is the human or bodily mechanism or body initiated."[20] The fetus, according to Ximeno, became "animated" once infused with a rational soul, but it was difficult to determine the moment after copulation when this occurred, although it was certainly present by forty days after conception in the case of males, and eighty days in the case of females.[21] In these texts, then, we see Mexican church officials both asserting their jurisdiction of rights with respect to the powers of the papacy and also following the directive of Gregory XIV, adopting a more moderate position toward abortion than that which Sixtus V's 1588 bull had pronounced.

Near the close of the next century, in 1679, Pope Innocent XI issued *Sanctissimus Dominus*, a text condemning sixty-five propositions that would incur excommunication if published or defended.[22] While his list covered a lot of territory, they included two that involved abortion: the thirty-fourth, that "it is lawful to procure an Abortion before the Conception is quickened, lest the Woman being discovered to be with Child should be either killed or defamed"; and the thirty-fifth, that "it seems probable that all Conceptions as long as they are in the Womb, are without a reasonable Soul; and that they then begin to have one when they are first born, and by consequence there is no Murder committed in any Abortion."[23] The Mexican Diocese published Innocent's text in 1684, and the Holy Office of the Inquisition universally designated the propositions as scandalous and dangerous. However, the tribunal never prosecuted their utterance (or enactment) as vigorously as it did various other religious crimes relating to sexuality, including bigamy and solicitation, which the court viewed as graver threats to social morality than abortion.

Historian Dolores Enciso observes that although the Catholic Church, in both papal decrees and individual confessionals, may have prohibited abortion as a form of homicide, it also allowed for exceptional circumstances in which homicide was permitted.[24] The catechism of the Council of Trent, influential in defining spiritual orthodoxy in viceregal Mexico, tolerated homicide in cases of "just wars," accidental homicide, or in self-defense. Likewise, homicide undertaken in the defense of familial honor was justified in both the viceregal and postindependence eras.

After Innocent XI's fairly obscure pronouncement, the papacy remained silent on abortion through the eighteenth and much of the nineteenth century, although individual theologians occasionally commented on the matter. These included, as Elizabeth O'Brien has discussed, Italian Jesuit and inquisitor Francesco Emanuele Cangiamila in his 1749 treatise calling for performance of the caesarean operation to extract fetuses from the uteruses of pregnant women at risk of death in order to secure their salvation.[25] O'Brien also uncovered a late eighteenth-century Limeño priest, Francisco González Laguna, who supported Cangiamila's initiative, arguing that embryos were animated from the moment of conception. However, she notes that contemporary physicians, including the Mexican doctor Antonio Medina, contested this claim. The timing of fetal ensoulment resurfaced within ecclesiastical pronouncements indirectly with Pope Pius IX's 1854 proclamation of Mary's Immaculate Conception, and explicitly with his 1869 bull *Apostolicae Sedis* in 1869, which revised the list of censures automatically imposed on offenders indicating that abortion merited excommunication at any stage of pregnancy.[26]

Many researchers, journalists, and advocates of the pro-life lobby cite Innocent's bull as an important turning point in the church's modern articulation of a hard-line anti-abortion position. Elizabeth O'Brien speculates, for example, that Mexican physicians rejected Pius's bull, which "enshrined life form the moment of conception" and provoked them into articulating a more medicalized definition of conception and gestation.[27] I contend, however, that this framing of Innocent's bull involves a distorted reconstruction of its purpose and content, perhaps because the complete text of this bull has not been published, as far as I have discovered, anywhere except in Latin.[28]

Apostolicae Sedis was not, at its core, a text aimed principally or exclusively at the issue of abortion. Rather, it was a piece of papal housekeeping whose purpose was to revise the list of censures invoked automatically in cases of grave sin and to identify papal jurisdiction over those acts that the Holy See alone reserved the power to absolve from excommunication and those that pertained to lower echelons of the church hierarchy. It covered forty-nine different acts, beginning with those most grievous sins that the papacy had the exclusive power to absolve. These included heresy, violent acts committed against officers of the church, forgers of apostolic documents, duelers, freemasons, and those who removed relics from cemeteries. In his bull Pius IX classified abortion in the much smaller category of lesser evils (along with clerics, regulars, or nuns who presumed to marry after having taken vows of chastity and those who knowingly used forged apostolic documents) that incurred excommunication over which bishops and ordinary priests might provide absolution. Not only was abortion nowhere near the headliner of *Apostolicae Sedis*, but the bull also classified it as a less grave sin than many others. Furthermore, its condemnation of abortion seems to have gone virtually unnoticed in Mexico. There is little discussion of the bull at the time of its proclamation, and those few articles that did refer to it focused on other elements, particularly its discussion of the Protestant heresy and the excommunication of freemasons.[29]

Popular instruction by the church on the sin of abortion was scarcer than it is in our day as well. Sermons and homilies in viceregal and nineteenth-century Mexico never treated such personal and intimate matters but more often events celebrated in the liturgical calendar. Abortion did feature in instructional catechisms and confessional guides, especially those directed at the indoctrination of Indigenous subjects, both in and after the viceregal era. Colonial catechisms briefly mentioned abortion in describing violations of the Fifth Commandment, including the act of "procuring an abortion for oneself or for another," although the fourth Provincial Council's catechism, published in 1772, specified that this was only a crime "when the fetus is not animated."[30] The council acknowledged that the subject of when animation occurred was a matter of contemporaneous debate, with extreme positions articulating that no soul existed in fetuses until birth, and others declaring animation occurred at conception.

Bartolomé de Alva's early seventeenth-century confessional in Nahuatl and Spanish instructed priests to ask their confessants "if they had taken some potion when they were pregnant to expel the criatura" and to question midwives whether "they had given some potion to an unmarried girl or pregnant person so that she would expel the criatura." In case of an affirmative answer, they were to admonish them that they had committed a grave sin, because the "criatura of God," would have died without receiving the "the means of its salvation, which is Holy Baptism."[31] Although abortion appeared in the confessional guide, this sin was overshadowed by the text's detailed instructions for policing the heresy of idolatry or monitoring such sexual practices as concubinage. Eighteenth-century midwifery guides, such as Antonio Medina's *Cartilla nueva util y necesaria* (New and necessary primer), originally published in Spain in 1750 but reprinted in Mexico in 1806, although condemning abortion nevertheless acknowledged the ambiguous status of some products of conception, as Elizabeth O'Brien notes, in Medina's reference to the product of early pregnancy as a "*molae* (roughly a 'mass')."[32]

In the colonial era, on the very rare occasions that discussions of abortion did come to the attention of the judges of the Mexican Inquisition, they were most often inclined to ignore the act. In one mid-seventeenth-century trial originating from the city of Puebla, the court investigated Isabel Hernández, a midwife and a curer, for witchcraft. Among the many clients Hernández described serving, she recounted one instance in which she had been retained by the family of a woman who was pregnant although understood publicly to be a virgin. When the woman went into labor, Hernández "gave to understand that what she suffered from was merely the detention of her menses, and that she would cure her with some powders."[33] Despite the indications that Hernández had supplied her client with a medicine to provoke a miscarriage, the court did not persist in any further questioning of her on the matter. Charges of inducing a miscarriage did not appear among the list of acts the court included in its accusation against the midwife.

The Inquisition's evident disinterest in pursuing cases in which women indicated they had pursued abortions characterizes the court's handling of other cases on the rare occasions when defendants confessed to having aborted fetuses under investigation for other religious crimes. One such instance involved María Marta de la Encarnación, a lay religious woman tried in 1717 for being a false mystic, practitioner of superstitions, and blasphemer. In his appearance before the court, de la Encarnación's father declared that, one year earlier, his daughter's menstruation had ceased, and "her belly rose." He had discussed these symptoms with his wife, who arranged that she should be bled from the heel, and this "caused Marta's belly to disappear."[34] A second witness described how de la Encarnación had told him that when she had realized she was pregnant, she resolved to "take something with which to provoke an abortion and get rid of the criatura."[35] Although de la Encarnación was convicted of being an *ilusa* (false mystic), abortion did not feature centrally in her sentence.

In an even more explicit example dating from 1731, Gregorio de Jesús María, a Carmelite priest, denounced himself before the court in Puebla de los Angeles. Referring to Pope Innocent's XI's 1679 decree, he confessed that he had provided a woman whom he had impregnated with "remedies to abort." Seeing that she was pregnant, he declared, "I looked for various remedies so that she could abort the pregnancy throughout the nine months."[36] On another occasion, he stated, he had given another woman a remedy for the same purpose. His self-denunciation never went further than his first declaration.[37] Despite papal and church council declarations about abortion's sinfulness, neither Mexico's secular ecclesiastical courts nor the tribunal of the Holy Office approached its prosecution with severity in the colonial period.

Condemnations of abortion appeared periodically in Catholic-oriented publications after independence. One 1849 article in the Catholic publication *La voz de la religión* (The voice of religion) enumerated abortion as one of the gravest injuries to God and humanity, along with the exposure of children (leaving newborns exposed to the elements), the "atrocious abuse of *patria potestad*," incestuous marriages, human sacrifice, the bloody spectacles of the circus, and other "disorders."[38] And in 1852 *El Siglo Diez y Nueve* (The nineteenth century) published a discourse about children by the bishop of Zacatecas, in which he referred to abortion as an act of homicide.[39] In one 1874 newspaper article treating the legality and morality of dueling, one Luis G. de la Sierra commented that fetuses could be considered human once they had quickened, and that "even the embryo, even the fetus that has just begun moving in the womb, should be the object of society's tender care."[40] However, the discussion of abortion in such venues was sporadic rather than constant, suggesting that, at midcentury, abortion did not figure prominently in the theological imaginations of Mexicans. But what about how the state envisioned abortion in criminal and legal terms in the premodern era?

Abortion Law to 1871

Both the provincial magistry and the legal experts populating the Sala del Crimen, the court judging criminal cases within New Spain's Real Audiencia (Royal Court), assessed criminal cases with reference to a large set of medieval and early modern Iberian codes and charters. These included the *Ordenamiento de Alcalá* (The orders of Alcalá, 1348), a royal code from Castile; various local charters including the *Fuero Real* (Royal charter, 1255); and *Las Siete Partidas* (The seven-part code, 1251–65). In the sixteenth century, the *Leyes de Toro* (Laws of Toro, 1505) and the *Recopilacón de Leyes de estos Reynos* (Compilation of the laws of these kingdoms, 1567) also became important legal sources. In 1805 King Charles IV's new collection of laws, the *Novísima Recopilación de las Leyes de España* (Newest compilation of the laws of Spain), was incorporated into this group.[41]

Independence from Spain brought few immediate changes to Mexico with respect to either the law's theoretical foundations or the administration of criminal justice. As was the case in much of Latin America, Mexico underwent a protracted, ten-year war for independence from Spanish rule between 1810 and 1821.[42] Participants from all of the racial groups and classes populating the viceroyalty fought on the side of independence, although greater numbers of *criollos* (people of Spanish descent born in the Americas) than *peninsulares* (Spaniards born in Iberia) tended to coalesce around the "patriots" who wished to sever ties with Spain. Various grievances prompted supporters to band behind the patriots' shifting leadership. These included economic complaints over recent tax hikes combined with population pressure, droughts, and inflation; critiques over the Bourbons' military mismanagement; dismay at the abdication of King Ferdinand VII at the time of the Napoleonic invasion; anger over the state's 1767 expulsion of the Jesuit order from Spanish America; resentment over peninsulares' near-monopoly on noble status; and Enlightenment-influenced demands for expanded popular sovereignty.

In the end more conservative and more radical factions fighting in the war negotiated a proclamation, the Plan of Iguala, which cemented 1821 Mexico's independence from Spain. This text declared that Mexico would become a Catholic constitutional monarchy, in which peninsulares and criollos (but not Indigenous people, African-descended Mexicans, or those of mixed race) would possess political and social equality. The new nation experienced a turbulent first three years of independence under the self-proclaimed "imperial" rule of Agustín de Iturbide but transitioned to a republic after Iturbide's 1824 arrest and execution.

Although colonial Mexicans expressed various quarrels with the Spanish state in the decades leading up to the war, most historians agree that these did not extend to dissatisfaction with the operation of the courts, institutions that Mexico's famously litigious Indigenous population had adopted on the heels of the Spanish Conquest of 1521, as venues in which to address complaints involving land encroachment and labor abuses, among others. Michael Scardaville, Brian Owensby, and Bianca Premo have all observed that colonial subjects, even those who were economically or politically marginalized, effectively used the courts of New Spain to advance their interests, restore order, and rectify wrongdoing.[43]

Perhaps for this reason—but also because of the political instability that characterized Mexico until the 1870s—the republican federal government did not move immediately to transform either the legal theory or the judicial practices governing abortion for fifty years after independence, until the issuance of the Federal District's 1871 penal code, adapted with few substantial changes by the other states in the Mexican union shortly thereafter.[44] Nineteenth-century works of *doctrina*, legal tracts summarizing and interpreting historic and current legal sources, such as Rafael Roa Bárcena's 1859 *Manual razonado de práctica criminal y medico-legal forense Mexicana* (Reasoned manual of Mexican criminal law and medical-legal forensics), ranked the legal codes Mexican justices should consider in formulating their sentences. Texts like this indicated that the Iberian legal codes central to the administration of justice in mid-nineteenth-century Mexico were the *Siete Partidas*, King Fernando III's thirteenth-century *Fuero juzgo* (Judicial charter), the fourteenth-century *Fuero viejo de Castilla* (Ancient charter of Castile), and the thirteenth-century *Fuero Real* (Royal charter).[45]

In practice, however, the only legal texts that first-instance judges trying abortion regularly cited in the first decades after independence were the *Siete*

Partidas or the oft-republished work of doctrina *Escriche*, first published in Mexico in 1837.[46] Occasionally judges referred to other Iberian or Mexican texts. Rarely these involved postindependence statutes from the federal or state governments. The *fiscal* (prosecutor) reviewing Yucatán midwife Bernarda Sulú's abortion trial at Mérida's superior court in 1854 requested that her trial be sent for review to a third-instance tribunal in conformity with the "law for the order of the administration of justice in the tribunals and courts of the common charter" issued by the federal minister of justice in December 1853.[47] In a second case originating in the town of Tehuacán, Puebla, in 1825, an assessor of the state's superior court advised the local *alcalde* (judge) investigating fifteen-year-old María Ambrosia for the crime of infanticide to strike a jury in order to judge the defendant as mandated by a state law passed one year earlier.[48]

More often judges explicitly cited early modern Iberian codes. The first-instance judge assessing charges against midwife Bernarda Sulú for abortion in Chocholá, Yucatán, in 1853, referred to passages from the *Fuero juzgo*, for example. Several of Sulú's clients had confessed that the Mayan midwife had provided them with drinks that provoked early miscarriages, at least one of which was of an animated fetus.[49] Sulú's judge cited laws 2 and 3 of the fourth title of book 6 of the *Fuero juzgo*, noting that the midwife deserved to be sentenced severely, since she had deprived life to at least two "innocent beings."[50] The specified passages in the *Fuero juzgo* discussed the administration of medicinal herbs to provoke abortions and treated the medicine's provider more harshly than the pregnant woman who ingested them. While a man gave herbs to a woman to abort should be put to death, a woman who took the herbs, "if she is a servant, she should receive two hundred lashings; if she is a free woman, she should forfeit her dignity and become a servant to the king."[51] Someone who caused the death of a pregnant woman in forcing her to abort should be executed, while those who caused the death of a fetus, but not of the woman who carried the fetus, should pay a larger or lesser fine, depending on whether or not the "child was formed."[52]

Along with consideration of the *Fuero juzgo*, Sulú's judges at both the first-instance and appellate levels referred extensively to particular passages of the *Siete Partidas*. As in many such cases, they cited the sections of the seventh *Partida* treating the crime of abortion (laws 4, 8, and 12, seventh title).[53] Law 4 decreed that those who killed should be less severely punished than with execution. Law 8 discussed the punishment appropriate to pregnant women who ate or drank "herbs known to provoke the expulsion of the criatura," specifying that, "if it was still alive," such acts merited capital punishment.[54] Law 8 also declared that if the criatura had not been alive, the pregnant woman should not be put to death, but merely banished for five years; the same punishment should be applied to a man who forced his wife to abort. However, if anyone other than her husband had forced the act, this person, should be killed. Law 12 discussed parricide, the murder of close family members, again declaring that those found guilty of such acts should be whipped publicly and then placed "in a leather sack along with a dog, a rooster, a snake, and a monkey, and, after having been enclosed with these four creatures, the sack should be sewn up and thrown into the sea or a nearby river."[55] Mexican judges throughout the nineteenth century referred to these passages from the *Partidas* in assessing reproductive crimes.[56] Although no woman in Mexico was put to death for the crime of abortion in either the viceregal or modern era, this colorful passage attracted devotees. Spanish physician Cristóbal Nieto de Peña, who published a tract on detecting the state of the fetus in the womb in the late eighteenth century, praised sixteenth-century Italian legal expert Julio Claro's reference to this passage.[57] And in one very unusual instance transpiring in late eighteenth-century Bogotá, Colombia, the Afro-descended, mixed-race woman María Santos, convicted of infanticide, was sentenced to "the death penalty by execution on the gallows in the accustomed public square, to which she will be conducted by the tail of a beast, and, after execution, she will be displayed for three hours on the gallows, and then will be enclosed in a chest on which will be painted a dog, a rooster, a monkey, and a snake, and this will be thrown into the closest river."[58]

Joaquin Escriche, author of the frequently cited work of doctrina of the same name, based his discussion of abortion on Iberian law used in the viceregal period, although his text did innovate from earlier positions in its limited support for inducing labor in cases when the health of pregnant women was threatened. The text adopted the *Partidas* as the definitive source on the crime, referring to harsher sentencing "if the fetus is already animated" and specifying that only intentional and fully realized abortion should be prosecuted.[59] *Escriche* also addressed the issue of whether doctors committed criminal acts by judging it expedient to intervene in pregnancies when either their completion or the act of birth threatened the life of a pregnant woman. The text commented that some experts supported the performance of risky caesarean birth in such situations, but others, including François-Emanuelle Fodéré (1764–1835), counseled abortion "because in this way it is possible to save the most precious of the two lives that might be lost."[60] *Escriche* suggested that the best course of action would be to await fetal development in the seventh month, when there was a higher possibility for the criatura to survive independently of the womb, and then to provoke premature labor.

Escriche also waded into the controversial issue of the distinction between the animated and nonanimated fetus. The text detailed the ancient tradition of identifying male animation as occurring at thirty days and female animation in a later period, described others' belief that animation occurred between the third and fourth months, still others who believed the soul only infused the baby at birth, and "the moderns" who situated animation at conception. The law, *Escriche* declared, was silent on this point, but he concluded that recent physiological discoveries suggested that conception and animation were simultaneous.[61]

In recommending how judges should evaluate both abortion and infanticide, *Escriche* also anticipated the particular manner in which Mexico's later penal codes dealt with these crimes in its discussion of the degree to which preserving familial honor should serve as a mitigating factor in assessing the crime's severity: "The woman who destroys the fruit of her womb to conserve her honor or her life or to not deliver the child into misfortune is not as guilty as she who commits this crime out of disgust for her husband."[62] *Escriche*, reflecting a sentiment typical of its day, and one that would endure long after it, asserted that the preservation of a woman's reputation for sexual chastity was often her most prized possession, conveying with it not only her own personal honor but also that of the men in her family who were charged with its safeguarding. As Sonya Lipsett-Rivera reminds us, women's reputation "was tied to their chastity as maidens and then their loyalty as wives and discrete respectability as widows."[63] Female sexual honor was more valuable than the corporal life of either fetus or newborn. Another contemporary popular work of doctrina, *Febrero*, echoed the same notion, describing the competing desires that might influence a pregnant young woman—"the love of a mother, or the sentiments of honor"—that might compel her to hide her pregnancy and the birth of her child. The text cited a contemporary verse:

> Two rulers Judge your fate,
> love winning over honor will bring you life,
> honor winning over honor will bring you death.[64]

Both *Escriche* and *Febrero* viewed abortion and infanticide as related to homicide. They specified that abortion was less a serious crime than homicide and, for this reason, judged that reclusion of varying lengths according to both the age of the fetus and the defendant was the act's appropriate punishment.

Although nineteenth-century justices referred to the imperative of sentencing abortionists to death, as discussed in the *Siete Partidas*, they more often referred to two different sections of the code when assessing these crimes. Law 12, title 14, of *Partida* 3 instructed judges that all criminal accusations must be proven by witness testimony or from knowledge possessed by the accuser but should never be founded on suspicion alone; all accusations must be proven and verified "by proof as clear as the light in which no doubt is possible."[65] Court officials in several trials referred to this article of the *Partidas*, both explicitly and abstractly.[66] In 1829, for instance, neighbors denounced Francisca Torres, a thirty-year-old single woman from Chiautla, Puebla, for ingesting medicines that provoked an abortion. After interviewing various eyewitnesses, the defendant herself, and midwives who had examined both her and the disinterred corpse of her baby, an assessor at Puebla's superior court commented that, although considerable evidence had been mounted against Torres, "to impose the death penalty, it is necessary to have proof as certain and clear as the light of mid day." In Torres's case, because he judged the evidence was not overwhelming, he recommended a sentence of four years' reclusion in a *recogimiento*, a correctional institution for wayward women.[67]

Law 8, title 31, of the seventh *Partida* addressed judges' requirement to sentence defendants appropriately according to their stations in life, as well as to the specific context in which the crimes occurred.[68] They should consider whether defendants were servants or free, noble or humble.[69] The *Partidas* advised that defendants of higher class should be punished in a more respectful manner than servants or members of the poorer classes. Those under ten and a half years of age should not be punished at all, and those under the age of seventeen should be sentenced with greater leniency than older defendants. Crimes occurring at night should be treated more harshly than those transpiring in daylight.[70] Judges often referred to this section of the *Partidas* when they sought to exercise their judicial discretion in order to exercise leniency in sentencing reproductive crimes. In the case of Yucatán midwife Bernarda Sulú's Indigenous clients, who confessed to having drunk the medicines with which she had provided them to provoke abortions, the court considered that, as members of the "Indigenous classes," they existed in a "deplorable state of rusticity" and so deserved its mercy.[71]

The Judicial History of Abortion to 1871

Catholic institutions, while formally prohibiting abortion, appeared in practice unconcerned with its commission through the viceregal period and first decades of the nineteenth century. In theory secular codes and instructional tracts approached abortion severely, but just as occurred in religious spheres, justices operating in criminal courts up until the 1870s often approached the assessment of abortion cases with marked indifference. When they did take notice of those accused of the crime and then convicted them for it, they did so with considerable leniency.

The holdings of nine archives, including the largest collection of colonial-era documents in Mexico, contain a mere four criminal investigations in ecclesiastical and criminal courts for the crime of abortion between 1521 and 1821, all occurring in central Mexico.[72] In the four colonial cases, one defendant, María Manuela Ramos, an Indigenous woman tried in in San Lorenzo Tultitlán in the modern-day state of Mexico in 1783, escaped from depósito before her case could be judged.[73] Matiana María, a second Indigenous woman from the same town, was tried the following year for having "aborted in a field and having left there the criatura, which was eaten by animals."[74] Matiana María claimed that she had not intentionally aborted but had miscarried alone, abandoned her criatura, and then sought refuge in the parish church of San Lorenzo. Although the judges of the Real Sala de Crimen had convicted Matiana María and sentenced her to six years' reclusion in the recogimiento Santa María Magdalena, the curate of San Lorenzo succeeded in having her released to him, since she had sought refuge in his church; he had her placed *en depósito* for an unspecified period instead. A third eighteenth-century case involving a military captain who had counseled a woman to ingest herbs to provoke an abortion was not pursued.[75] The final eighteenth-century case against Juana Trinidad Márquez is detailed in this chapter's opening pages. In none of these cases did judges refer to any of the legal codes discussed earlier that theoretically outlawed the practice of abortion.

It seems preposterous to conclude that the absence in viceregal Mexico of community members who denounced women for abortion, or of legal authorities who prosecuted them for the crime, indicates that women were not aborting unwanted fetuses in this period. This is unlikely, given the prevalence of both persons of expertise and medicines available to women who wished to abort. In addition it seems unlikely, given the judicial evidence, that Mexican women simply began aborting their pregnancies with far greater frequency in the late nineteenth century. We also know that women in other parts of the Americas and Europe at this time engaged in the practice in much higher numbers. For the early modern period, it is virtually impossible to trace with precision the rates of abortion. However, recent scholarship on both the Americas and western Europe suggests both that purgative medicines and surgeries were widely available to, and ubiquitously used by, women in this era, and also that the crime was much more widely tolerated by the public and by courts than scholars than heretofore understood.[76] As Elizabeth Dore has observed was the case in terms of women's financial autonomy in particular, this was one way in which the legal and social changes of the liberal era did not necessarily imply improved circumstances for women.[77]

There are some indications that women practiced abortion in the colonial era and early nineteenth century more frequently than criminal cases suggest. First, despite the widespread attribution of Mexican women's soaring fertility across time, some details from the historical record suggest a different reality. As I pointed out in earlier scholarship, historian Silvia Arrom, in her examination of 141 Mexico City wills dating from 1802 to 1855, discovered that "over 14 per cent had given birth to no children at all by age forty-five; a further 17 per cent had borne only one child, while another 15 per cent had only had two children."[78] One of Arrom's subjects, a doña Salvadora Lavanes, observed that "during our marriage we had no children whatsoever despite the many years we were married."[79] Some of the couples in Arrom's sample might have been infertile, but others no doubt actively regulated their reproduction through contraception or abortion.

Medical, religious, and legal texts also indicate that abortion was more widespread than criminal records indicate. Midwifery tracts circulating in the late eighteenth century, including Ignacio Segura's *Avisos saludables a las parteras* (Healthy advice to midwives, 1775) and Antonio Medina's *Cartilla nueva util y necesaria para instruirse las matronas* (New and necessary primer for the instruction of midwives, 1750, 1806), admonished midwives for providing contraception or provoking abortions in their clients. Judicial administrators and governors also lamented what they described as women's widespread practices of inducing miscarriages or murdering newborns. Viceregal officials declared as much in the public outcry surrounding the discovery in the streets of Popotla, a town outside of the capital, of a group of four or five newborn corpses in 1818. The news prompted a state investigation into the frequency of infanticide and the accessibility of *casas de expósitos* (institutions housing abandoned children) to women across the viceroyalty.[80]

Despite such indications of abortion's occurrence in late colonial and early republican Mexico, the lack of judicial concern with abortion in the viceregal era extended for the first five decades after independence. From 1821 up until the passage of the Federal District's penal code of 1871, courts in central Mexico, Oaxaca, and Yucatán processed a total of only eleven abortion cases, the majority in Yucatán and Oaxaca, finding defendants guilty of the crime in only four cases. Judges were reluctant to convict because it was difficult for them to be absolutely certain that defendants had voluntarily aborted. First, medicinally induced early miscarriages could occur in privacy, so the act normally had no witnesses. Second, accidental miscarriage was in this period—as is still the case—a normal and frequent occurrence. While data does not exist on historic miscarriage rates in Mexico, we do know that, internationally, at present, 15 percent of all pregnancies typically miscarry in the first trimester.[81] If anything it is likely this rate would have been significantly higher in the past. Infant and neonatal mortality rates were even higher than this. In the eighteenth century, for instance, 25 percent of the population did not live beyond the first year of life.[82] All of these factors meant that it was rare for courts to find defendants guilty of abortion unless they confessed to it. In several of these cases, defendants suspected of voluntary or intentional abortion asserted that they had unintentionally miscarried after having been physically assaulted by someone who did not intend to provoke an abortion, and the courts normally granted them the benefit of the doubt.[83]

In other instances their peers denounced young, unmarried, and poor women for having ingested medicinal remedies that provoked early labor. In the 1829 trial of Francisca Torres, of Chiautla, Puebla, the accused confessed to having taken the pungent herb epazote but said she had only done this to remedy her "menstrual detention." Several witnesses asserted that Torres had physically resisted examination by a midwife in the days leading up to her labor and declared that her baby had been stillborn.[84] A midwife called to testify provided details about various other medicines she had given to Torres, intending, she said, only to address her "detention of the blood." But the remedies she had supplied her with included herbs like *altamisa* and *manzanilla* (chamomile), both plants women had long used to provoke miscarriages.[85] Torres was imprisoned for nearly three years while the court at both the local and superior levels considered her case, interrogating her again in March 1832. In November 1832 the local *alcalde* convicted Torres, while the superior court judge who reviewed her case, citing the severity of the *Siete Partidas*'s view of abortion, confirmed her sentence of four years' imprisonment. The state supreme court that reviewed her case the following year, however, recommended reducing her sentence because the evidence presented against Torres was inconclusive. Before this could happen, however, Torres died in the midst of an epidemic that swept the hospital in which she had been confined.

Criminal courts opened five abortion cases in Yucatán between 1853 and 1863. Four defendants—midwife Bernarda Sulú, two of her clients, and one accomplice—were investigated in one 1853 trial. Although Sulú was found guilty and sentenced to six years of hospital service, she escaped custody and never served any portion of her sentence. Her two clients, both of whom confessed to having imbibed concoctions she had given them to induce early labor, were both condemned to between three and four years hospital service.[86] In three of the other four cases from the 1850s and 1860s, judges dismissed the cases or absolved defendants of the crime, citing the absence of definitive evidence, including in one case in which a man charged that midwife Concepción Coronel was responsible for the deaths of his wife and their infant.[87] In the final case, a judge of the superior court in Mérida commented that the charge of intentional abortion against Pastoral Quintal "could not be sustained by the rigor of the law for such a serious crime." A first-instance judge in her case had ruled that since the allegations against her had not been entirely dismantled, she should nevertheless serve a short sentence of four months' service in the city's General Hospital to encourage her to mend her ways. The upper court upheld the ruling.[88]

In the state of Oaxaca, we know little about the circumstances of another woman absolved of suspicion of having voluntarily aborted in the capital city in 1842, other than her name—Arcadia Martínez—and that the judge of the second court room of the state superior court absolved her, citing law 12, title 14, of the third *Partida* and law 26, title 1, of the seventh *Partida* because he found the evidence against her insufficient.[89] In Oaxaca's northwestern judicial district of Huajuapan, courts opened a further two abortion cases in 1826 and 1849, but local judges found neither defendant guilty.[90]

Although there was a slight uptick in investigations and convictions for abortion in the first five decades after independence, as compared to during the colonial era, neither courts nor community members demonstrated a noticeable preoccupation with the crime. Few cases were denounced, and judges did not pursue most denunciations. The absence of interest in abortion is particularly apparent if we compare the prosecution of this crime to the rate at which it was denounced and prosecuted in the closing decades of the nineteenth century (to be discussed in the next chapter) and to courts' contemporaneous prosecution of other crimes. In Oaxaca, for instance, the archival subseries containing criminal trials for the district of Teposcolula in the nineteenth century contains over three thousand files; over two hundred treat homicide, but none involve abortions.[91] Similarly, in Yucatán, in the same period during which the state supreme court pursued five criminal investigations for abortion, it initiated over six hundred investigations for homicide.[92] Judges were little inclined to convict defendants for abortion, a crime whose occurrence was notoriously difficult to demonstrate with the absolute certainty of evidence as law 12, title 14, of the third *Partida* instructed, as clear as the light of day. What is even more striking about the low numbers of criminal cases for abortion before 1871 is the absence of peer denunciations for the crime despite the evidence that women continued to take medicinal abortifacients throughout this era.

Medical Practices from the Pre-Columbian Period to 1871

Although women's practices of abortion were only partly visible, we can find indications that midwives, herbalists, healers, and laywomen possessed extensive knowledge about abortion across this long time period, and that its practice was ubiquitous. Before the late nineteenth century, almost all abortions were medicinal; they involved women's ingestion of herbs, flowers, and other plants that provoked early miscarriages. Rarely did discussion of method of provoking abortion other than the ingestion of abortifacients precede the late nineteenth century, although physician José Ferrer Espejo did comment in his 1854 lectures "Obstetrical Lessons" that abortions could also be induced by "those criminal manoeuvrings that women used to make themselves abort" or "by engaging in violent exercise or by ingesting harmful drinks."[93] Knowledge about medicinal abortifacients derived from all three geographical origins of viceregal society: Mesoamerica, early modern and medieval Iberia, and Africa.

Few sources survive documenting African women's use of reproductive medicines in the Americas, although we do know of African women's use of medicinal abortificacients, particularly the "peacock flower" *Poinciana pulcherrima* (a plant native to Mexico) in the Antilles and Caribbean coast that African women used to induce abortions in both Barbados and Surinam.[94] Pre-Hispanic and early postcontact sources document the extensive gynecological expertise and sophisticated botanical expertise of Indigenous midwives, or *ticitl*. Their realm of expertise included bone setting, bleeding, purging, closing wounds, and knowing the medicinal properties of herbs, roots, and minerals. In the mid-sixteenth century, Franciscan missionary Bernardino de Sahagún's Indigenous informants explained that midwives had extensive botanical knowledge of medicines that could either induce early miscarriages or facilitate labor in full-term pregnancies, and that they knew how to manipulate the uterus to change the position of the fetus externally in order to facilitate birth.[95] Once labor began, midwives gave a pregnant woman a bath in the *temazcalli* (sweat lodge), "and after the bath, gave them to drink the root of a crushed herb called *cihuapatli* that has the property of impelling or pushing out the criatura."[96] If labor pains persisted for too long, they might also administer "the powdered dried tail of an animal called the *tlacuatzin* [an opossum]. And with this, she would give birth more easily."[97]

Physician and naturalist Francisco Hernández, the first Protomédico of the Indies, also produced a detailed record of the medicines and capabilities of Indigenous midwives during his seven-year exploration of the viceroyalty's botanical wealth, beginning in 1570. Although intentional abortion was a crime punishable by death in pre-Columbian society, Hernández, Sahagún, and other writers described plants that Indigenous populations used to induce menstruation. In addition to *cihuapatli*, Hernández cataloged the *huitzilxochitl* tree, which "provoked menstruation," and the plants *curutzeti*, *holquautil*, and *tlilxochitl* (vanilla), which did likewise.[98] The latter, when mixed with the herb *mecaxóchitl*, "shortened labor and helped to expel the afterbirth and the dead criatura."[99] Elsewhere he commented that both *xalquhuitl* and the *cococaquilitl* flower "provoked menstruation."[100] He also described the efficacy of the *yauhtli* (a perennial flower) to "stimulate menstruation, provoke abortion and expel dead fetuses" and listed other labor accelerators: *miahoapatli* (an herb), the root of the *phehuame*, and *tlaquuquétzal*, which "as an aromatic smoke, or suppository, or taken in any liquid form" accelerated birth.[101]

Hernández, like Sahagún, gathered his information from Indigenous informants and texts, including the work of Mattinus de la Cruz and Juannes Badianus, who had composed the first Latin-Nahuatl illustrated botanical treatise, the *Badianus Manuscript* (Codex Barberini), in 1552. Their text included a discussion of a "remedy for recent parturition," which prescribed the ingestion of *cihuapatli* crushed in water, the small stone *eztetl*, and the tail of the *tlacuatzin*, all of which would provoke delivery if labor was stalled.[102] Several other sixteenth-century missionaries and chroniclers, including Gonzalo Fernández de Oviedo and Toribio de Benavente Motolonía, likewise noted the existence of medicines that might provoke miscarriages, and women expert in administering them.[103]

Medical texts, criminal and inquisition trials, and other sources document that knowledge of these early colonial abortifacients endured though the colonial period and the nineteenth century. One of the earliest abortion records that historians have located involved a Sinaloan woman, Isabel de Ovando, who self-denounced to the Holy Office of the Inquisition in 1627 because she had requested an abortifacient for her daughter from an Indigenous healer.[104] In his 1788 *Compendio de la medicina*, physician Juan Manuel Venegas discussed various treatments that could restore a woman's "suppressed" menses. One cure that he suggested was drinking an infusion of the chamomile flowers; a second was a soak in a hot hip bath (*semicupio*) infused with lavender, or the herbs mugwort and pennyroyal and the malva and juniper flowers.[105] The eighteenth-century scientific writer Antonio León y Gama commented in a tract he composed in 1795 that "all the uterine illnesses from which women suffer can be cured by the multitude of herbs known by the generic name of *cihuapatli*, or medicine of women." He also observed that as ubiquitous a product as *pulque* (a popular fermented cactus drink) could be drunk to "provoke menstruation in women."[106] Anthropologist Saydi Núñez Cetina explains that both *cihuapatli* and another labor stimulator, *cuernecillo de centeno* (ergot), operated by inducing contractions in the uterus and impeding uterine-placental circulation, causing the death of the fetus by asphyxiation, followed by its expulsion.[107]

Women's use of such medicines continued in the postindependence era, although medical authorities increasingly viewed them with suspicion. The medical faculty of Michoacán published a midwifery manual in 1857 that commented that labor accelerators like altamisa and *zihuapatzli* (an alternative spelling of *cihuapatli*) "are very dangerous and should only be used in special cases."[108] The most prominent obstetrician of the period, Juan María Rodríguez, however, expressed cautious approval of the use of cihuapatli in the 1878 edition of his canonical text, the *Guía clínica del arte de los partos* (Clinical guide of the art of childbirth), commenting that an extract of the flower might be used after the expulsion of the placenta to prevent hemorrhaging.[109] Late nineteenth-century medical texts, from within Mexico and beyond it, acknowledged the effectiveness of the plant. The first Pan-American Medical Congress published the findings of Mexican physician Fernando Altamirano in 1894, commenting that cihuapatli, once digested, "produced strong uterine contractions."[110]

We do not possess records of Mayan medical knowledge before the eighteenth century. However, late colonial sources, as well as more recent ethnobotanical tracts, record similar information about Mayan knowledge of naturally occurring abortifacients. One anonymous 1805 botanical text from the Yucatán described some "plants that grew under water, that fishermen called *Ybinhá* or foam of the water, and that dried and ground up and given in wine to women would re-establish their menstruation; some of them aborted by accident or by evil intent."[111] The same text also described another plant: "*Cullo*, which is found in the mountains around the city of *Tismin* [Tizimín], produces a very effective stimulant, which is useful to women experiencing the retention of menstruation, and the pains that these can provoke."[112]

In many of these sources, authors referred to a belief that was also common to medieval and early modern European thought: ingestion of medicines to provoke a miscarriage was unlawful and unsanctioned, but the ingestion of medicines to "regularize the menses" was perfectly licit, even though identical medicines were used for both objectives. In Mexico, as was also true in medieval and early modern Europe, according to John Riddle, "most authorities did not consider the taking of a menstrual regulator, regardless of whether there was a pregnancy, as an abortifacient."[113] European women from the classical period onward had effectively used a variety of plants as both emmenagogues and abortifacients, including pennyroyal, rue, and savin (juniper), cotton root, and *artemisia* (mugwort), called *altamisa* in Mexico.[114] Technically, as Ann Hibner Koblitz details, "an emmenagogue is a substance that brings on (delayed) menstruation whether or not it was pregnancy that caused the missed period, whereas an abortifacient destroys the fertilized ovum and/or causes the uterine lining in which the embryo has been implanted to be expelled."[115] In practice, however, the distinction between these actions would have been undetectable to most historical actors treated in this book, no matter the century in which they lived.

Colonial and nineteenth-century Mexicans drew intellectual, legal, and cultural distinctions between licit "menstrual regulation" and illicit "abortion," but they also frequently used the same medicines and practices to effect both ends. State-supported publications provided legitimacy to the practice of lawfully regulating one's menses. A 1795 edition of the *Gazeta de México*, one of the viceroyalty's earliest news periodicals and a mouthpiece of the modernizing Bourbon state, published a remedy consisting of a mixture of the reduction of the herb *viperina*, mixed with wine, cream of tartar, and two spoonfuls of quina leaves that produced a medicine to treat various ailments including chronic chest illness and the suppression of the menses.[116] Viceregal and nineteenth-century medical treatises and guides for *boticarios* (pharmacists) similarly described various remedies that could provoke menstruation. One collection of various medicinal recipes dating from about 1790 contained a recipe for "herb water made of juniper and mugwort" to be given for three consecutive mornings that served "well to bring down menstruation."[117]

Discussions of the ingestion of medicines to lawfully regularize suspended menstruation appear frequently in criminal trials of women accused of the crimes of both abortion and infanticide in the viceregal era and the nineteenth century. In Francisca Torres's 1829 trial for abortion, originating in Chiautla, Puebla, a midwife testified that she had provided a medicine containing *alfolba* (fenugreek), chamomile, elderberry flower, and malva, but she asserted that the cure was aimed to cure the "*detención de luna*" (menstrual detention) and not pregnancy.[118] Likewise, in María de la Luz López's 1851 infanticide trial, a doctor who had attended to the defendant during her pregnancy declared he had prescribed baths in garlic to treat what he judged to be simply her menstrual detention.[119] Another woman, tried for infanticide in Carmen, Yucatán, in 1865 admitted that she had taken *aceite de higuerilla* (castor oil) shortly before miscarrying her fetus, a substance that current-day research documents can operate as an abortifacient.[120]

In some cases medical treatises alluded to the fact that medicines might induce miscarriage and advised pregnant women to avoid them. One anonymous 1785 pharmacists' manual, *Prontuario o método fácil en donde se contienen las mas eficaces Medicinas* (Handbook or simple method in which is contained the most efficient medicines), included a description of a medicine called the "life water of women." While not providing the ingredients of the concoction, the text warned against pregnant women taking it. Another remedy, the "water of the embryo," could ostensibly facilitate labor.[121] While neither remedy indicated its purpose the intentional induction of miscarriages, it is, of course, possible that boticarios or their clients would have purposed such medicines to this end.

Criminal trials from various locations in Mexico document that pregnant women, midwives, pharmacists, physicians, and judicial officers all continued to accept women's use of medicines to regularize suspended menses through the nineteenth century. This is apparent, for example, in the infanticide trial of Petra Sevilla, a young woman who worked as a *pilmama* (nursemaid) on a large estate in the state of Puebla in 1836. Sevilla was accused of having thrown her newborn in the *communes* (latrine) after giving birth. The owners of the estate had called physician don José Mariano Rivadenegra to treat her when she complained of pain in her belly, and he had prescribed some herbs. Rivadenegra testified that those living on the estate had informed him they had not known whether she suffered from a miscarriage or abortion or the "breaking of a detained menstruation," but since he had seen no signs of a newborn and had not been ordered to determine if she had just given birth, he merely prescribed a medicine for blood flow.[122] The details of another criminal trial, this one for infanticide, were summarized in Mexico City's daily newspaper *Siglo Diez y Nueve* in November 1852. A young woman called Vicenta Bonilla, facing an undesired pregnancy, sought assistance from a doctor, Domingo Figueroa, "under the pretext of having a painful inflammation of the belly."[123] Figueroa, whether realizing she was pregnant or not, prescribed some medicines that immediately stimulated the onset of Bonilla's labor.

Courts sometimes acknowledged that menstrual suspension was a likely indicator of pregnancy, as occurred in María Juana's 1855 infanticide trial originating in Huaquechula, Puebla. The trial was initiated when a townsperson discovered the corpse of a newborn that animals had mangled. After interrogating several town residents, the court identified María Juana, who at first acknowledged her recent pregnancy, as the guilty party. During her second interview, she denied the pregnancy and suggested that many of her neighbors had recently been pregnant, implying that any one of them might have been the responsible party. In his instructions to the local judge about the witness interrogation he should undertake, a legal advisor from Puebla's superior court advised that the judge should question all the defendant's neighbors, but especially the women, "who were knowledgeable about the illnesses and afflictions of their sex, to have them declare what they knew about these and about their own experiences of menstrual retention."[124] Subsequently, the local judge questioned numerous female witnesses about not only whether they had any knowledge of the defendant's medical status vis-à-vis menstrual detention but also about whether or not they had experienced such a state. Micaela Ventura told the court she knew nothing about the case because she had been at home sick for several months and added "that she has never retained her menstruation and for this reason, she is ignorant of the effect such a state could produce."[125] A second woman declared that she had often observed the defendant in public and "had never seen that she looked pregnant; and since her own menstruation has never been suspended, she cannot explain what might cause such an occurrence."[126] Any woman who asserted she had experienced menstrual detention might have been suspected of having given birth in secret, but here all of them denied having experienced such a state. At the end of this case, as was common to most, the grounds for demonstrating the commission of infanticide were not sufficiently certain, and María Juana was convicted only of having abandoned the corpse of her stillborn infant.

Community Attitudes to Abortion and to Female Sexuality

As well as resulting in a nonconviction, María Juana's 1855 trial was typical of many others from this period in that her peers did not initiate a case against her out of suspicions drawn from their observations about her sexual or reproductive practices. Instead a local court initiated a case against her only once the public discovery of her newborn's corpse rendered an investigation into the circumstances of its death inevitable. Widely held attitudes toward reproduction, motherhood, and female sexuality contributed to the climate determining that few community members denounced their peers for the crime of abortion in the period before the last decades of the nineteenth century. Before this era the Mexican populace treated childbirth as a private matter that lay outside the purview of respectable medicine, scientific scrutiny, and public discourse.[127] In the viceregal era and through the first half of the nineteenth century, midwives and other unlicensed practitioners delivered most babies born in Mexico. Obstetrical medicine, although it started to be taught in midwifery centers in the 1830s and 1840s, did not become a respected branch of medicine until the 1870s, with the foundation of the obstetrical clinic in the capital's Casa de Maternidad in 1870 and the foundation of a *cátedra* (professorship) in gynecology at the Escuela de Medicina in 1887.

Childbirth was not a matter of concern for either members of the public, or for state officials, but only for pregnant and laboring women and those who attended them at birth. Even these figures, in the scant surviving descriptions that allude to these moments in court transcripts, represented childbirth as a commonplace event, unworthy of public acknowledgment or attention. Often poor Mexican women did not have the luxury of temporal or spatial resources required to mark the significance of childbirth; when they mentioned giving birth in their testimonies, they depicted it as an unremarkable affair sandwiched between their other demanding daily obligations. For example, in her 1838 testimony in an infanticide investigation in the town of San Jerónimo las Caleras, Puebla, María del Carmen Camila narrated that, "at nine in the morning on the twentieth [of the month], she gave birth to a little girl in one of the alfalfa fields near the mill and she left her alive covered by some grasses, until about five in the afternoon." She was only able to return to the field and check on her newborn after finishing her day's work in the mill.[128] Another defendant, María Rosalia, investigated for infanticide in Tepeaca, Puebla, in 1856 declared that she had miscarried her infant moments after arriving home from gathering firewood, as she did nearly every day.[129]

Routine childbirth was an unremarkable occasion for many. Criminal trials also demonstrate that during the viceregal period and for the five decades following it, abortion was a not a crime of grave moral concern to neighbors, family members, and employers. Rarely in this body of trials did any witnesses pass moral judgment on women investigated for inducing abortions. In one exceptional case, from Chiautla, Puebla, in 1829, the first-instance judge trying defendant Francisca Torres, accused of having imbibed medicines to induce a miscarriage, asked the defendant "to account for why she had been motivated to take medicine to abort, when she must have known that this would have meant she would send her criatura to limbo."[130] The magistrate here confirmed that the chief theological and judicial preoccupation of the period respecting abortion lay not, as became the case in the late twentieth century, with the idea that the act of conception endowed the fetus with a human life. Instead the judge's comment reveals his era's preoccupation with the imperative to baptize all fetuses before death to ensure their rescue them from eternal damnation.[131]

This notion lay behind early modern texts' instruction that birth attendants should insert a syringe of holy water into birth canal of women undergoing difficult births to baptize fetuses at risk of dying.[132] It also prompted eighteenth-century theological and medical directives that all birth attendants—physicians, midwives, and even priests—be prepared to perform the caesarean operation in cases in which laboring women risked death, in order to ensure fetal baptisms.[133] This idea also explained why contemporary accounts of difficult births, including those of triplets, published in the *Gazeta de México* carefully cataloged details about newborn baptisms. Such notices, like the following 1795 example from Acapulco, might describe the demise of newborn as joyous occasions, as long as baptism preceded death: "On the 23rd of the month just passed María Marcela Martínez, a single, free *parda* [woman of mixed Black and Spanish descent] . . . gave birth with good fortune to three criaturas, all male, and who were named in Holy Baptism Joseph Miguel María, Miguel María, and Vicente María. The birth was most extraordinary because of the diversity of colors presented in the criaturas, since one of them appeared to be Spanish, another Indian, and the other Black. On the 25th, they all died, and it is unknown if the mother has faced any ill effects to date."[134]

The contemporary devotion to ensuring the salvation of newborns' souls notwithstanding, the instance of Francisca Torres's judge lecturing her on the threat she had posed to the soul of her newborn was exceptional. It was unusual for contemporary observers to remark upon either the physical or spiritual health of infants. Although individual families no doubt mourned infant deaths in their households, the aggressive mortality rates in eighteenth-century foundling homes suggests that community—but especially state—estimation for the value of newborns' lives, especially those born in poor households, was not high. In its first eight years of operation, the capital city's late eighteenth-century home for abandoned children, the Casa de Niños Expósitos, received 619 children; 415 of them died in infancy.[135] While protecting criaturas' souls through religious rites may have been a contemporary priority, safeguarding their material well-being, whether before or after birth, was not.

Community members who gave evidence in late colonial and nineteenth-century criminal trials sometimes made pronouncements about the immorality of women who engaged in infanticide, but this, too, was exceptional rather than typical. María de los Santos Vazquez, a neighbor who denounced María Ix in Tical, Yucatán, in 1857, described Ix as a "bad woman" who had smothered and surreptitiously buried her newborn.[136] The coworker of María Juana, the young woman who confessed to having exposed her newborn in an alfalfa field, was aghast to learn of this and declared "that for this deed God would punish us and we would no longer have food to eat."[137] These witnesses condemned the idea of killing newborns. However, community members uttered no such judgments about women accused of committing abortion, either because accidental miscarriages were so common that nobody was ever certain the acts had been intentional, or because they only considered the act a crime once a fetus had separated from its mother through the act of birth.

Some criminal trials suggest Mexicans' assent, at least up until the mid-nineteenth century, to the notion that pregnant women might choose to publicly present pregnancies as simply cases of "menstrual detention." In one 1842 infanticide trial from Huauchinango, Puebla, for example, a neighbor described her interaction with the defendant, María Rosa del Carmen, who had been denounced for having suffocated her newborn. Del Carmen's neighbor testified that she had long known del Carmen was pregnant. However, on the day of the infant's death, she declared that she had conversed with her neighbor, asking if "her detention of menstruation had ceased." Elaborating, the woman said that although she had known del Carmen was pregnant, "she did not ask her about it, nor communicate it to anyone for fear that this would mean she [del Carmen] would lose her public credit."[138] Her approach to perceiving but not acknowledging her neighbor's pregnancy, which she instead referred to as "menstrual detention," suggests she understood that reproductive matters as the concern of her neighbor alone.

Community members refrained from denouncing their peers to criminal courts for committing abortion before the late nineteenth century. However, by midcentury, they began expressing more pointed preoccupations with the sexual lives and sexual honor of plebeian women, a preoccupation that was notably less pronounced in the viceregal period. Elite discourses about the imperative of female virginity and chastity, no doubt, had a much older history, but such preoccupations were much stronger in those sectors for whom such states was connected to the maintenance of *limpieza de sangre* (cleanliness of the blood) and the inheritance of nobility to legitimate heirs. Proscriptive literature in the viceregal era mandated the strict maintenance of female sexual purity and abhorrence for sexual practices beyond reproductive intercourse that occurred within sanctified marriage. However, as Sonya Lipsett-Rivera has recently commented, "community understanding of acceptable conduct by a couple often showed a healthy respect for or ignorance of the rules and a greater tolerance for behavior outside the norm than was reflected in the official discourse."[139] The wide gap that existed between the model of sexual purity and the reality of alternative practices is evident, among other places, in New Spain's extremely high rates of illegitimacy. Pilar Gonzalbo Aizpuru has uncovered that these reached over 50 percent of the *casta* population in urban communities in the eighteenth century.[140]

In the late colonial period and early nineteenth century, non-elite Mexicans associated female honor with various attributes. Richard Boyer observed that in the late colonial era, plebeians showed they were honorable by, among other things, displaying their adherence to Christianity, by deferring to elders and exhibiting control over emotions.[141] As Laura Shelton has found, in the early nineteenth-century northern frontier regions, *buenas costumbres* (good customs) included demonstrations of sexual virtue and obedience to parents or husbands and behavior that contributed broadly to serve the "common good."[142] In earlier scholarship I traced how their peers associated women's honor through their membership in Christian, tax-paying families, their reputations for hard work, and their obedience to their parents.[143] By midcentury, however, witnesses in criminal cases more often discussed female honor more frequently with reference to sexual virtue specifically. By then plebeian Mexican women in Mexico testified to criminal courts in their trials for infanticide and abortion that they subscribed to the notion that the maintenance of their reputations for sexual purity was imperative to the defense of familial honor. In fact this proved a much stronger consideration than contemporary concerns with the life or health of either fetuses or newborn babies. While most women accused of aborto denied they had intentionally provoked abortions, some accused of infanticide justified their behavior by explaining they had been motivated to out of fear of punishment by their male family members, or, less frequently, their mothers or grandmothers. Such punishment, when inflicted, could be harsh. In her infanticide investigation, originating in Maxcanú, Yucatán, in 1895, defendant Victoria Zapata told her sister that she would "tell the truth even though her father might kill her for it, that it was she who had given birth to the criatura and that she did it out of the fear that she had of her father for this sin that she had committed out of her weakness."[144]

Beginning in the mid-nineteenth century, family members as well as municipal authorities began denouncing with greater frequency women whose sexual or reproductive practices they suspected. For example, in 1844 Fernando Mendoza, a lay assistant to a parish priest in the small town of Coixtlahuaca, Oaxaca, took it upon himself to confront a young woman whom he said he had observed to be pregnant and then was suddenly and inexplicably pregnant no longer. Mendoza, who declared he had been tasked with the role of "keeping vigil" over the behavior of women in the town, informed both the chief constable and a justice of the peace about her state and urged them to investigate her on charges of abortion or infanticide.[145]

The contemporary condemnation of women who disobeyed or deceived male family members is also illustrated in the case of the Mayan woman, Paulina Uc, convicted of infanticide in the city of Campeche in 1865. The fiscal who assessed Uc's case in Yucatán's supreme court requested that its judges award her with the harshest available sentence of ten years' imprisonment because he found the circumstances of Uc's case particularly disturbing. Her alleged action of smothering her newborn was no different from those in many other cases. Uc inspired the wrath of her judge not because of her actions against her infant, but because she had deceived her husband into marrying her when she had known she was pregnant with another man's baby and had then killed her newborn child to prevent her unsuspecting husband from learning of the child's existence.[146]

For these defendants, their peers, and their judges, the social value of the preservation of women's reputations for sexual honor and their manifestation of obedience to their parents and spouses was greater than the social cost of women's engagement in a violent crime, or the human cost of the lost life of the newborn baby or fetus. While court officials and other witnesses sometimes discussed the immorality of mothers who murdered, actors in these trials do not consider the value of the lost lives of newly born babies. Finally, the paucity of denunciations for the crime of abortion before the late nineteenth century suggests that a shift may have occurred in terms of the scrutiny of sexual honor, from an era of greater acceptance of female self-regulation in the earlier era, to a period of increased social scrutiny by peers as the nineteenth century progressed. In ways they had not done earlier, by the closing decades of the century, Mexicans who occupied lower positions on the social hierarchy devalued their acquaintances, family members, and employees when they lost their sexual honor.

Conclusion

The performance and prosecution of abortion remained relatively unchanged between the viceregal period and the first five decades after independence. The ingestion of plant-based abortifacients was the method women used most frequently to abort fetuses. Abortion may have been banned by law, but various sources show that women engaged in it ubiquitously, often under guise of merely practicing licit "menstrual regulation." The 1806 viceregal decrees calling for the establishment of a "department of secret births" within the Mexico City Poor House where women could give birth anonymously and depart with their honor intact declared that the institution was necessary because of the frequency with which women either killed their newborns or "used powerful abortives."[147] However, few people denounced others for the crime, and courts rarely convicted defendants for it.

Several factors explain the state, the church, and the public's lack of preoccupation with abortion. Contemporary religious beliefs prioritized the assurance of baptism over the loss of fetal or newborn life. From a medical standpoint, natural miscarriages were so frequent it was difficult to detect the difference between these and intentional abortions. In this early period, the public also articulated its acceptance of the notion that reproductive choices lay within the purview of individual women, rather than public institutions. The moral scrutiny of plebeian women's sexual practices also seems to have been more relaxed than it became in later periods. One explanation for this is that this era preceded the emergence of Mexico's feminist movement, hence long before the emergence of a discourse supporting and celebrating women's self-determination. In the twentieth century, when feminists advocated for women's rights to sexual and economic autonomy, some saw such ideas as threatening to the stability of the family and thus as a threat to broader social stability. Fear of female independence became a reason for condemning abortion. However, in the viceregal era and the early nineteenth century, before the emergence of a discourse of female autonomy, no provocation existed for the emergence of a counterdiscourse championing the sanctity of the family and abortion's threat to its status. Many of these circumstances would change in the decades following the 1871 passage of the Federal District's first criminal code and its subsequent adoption in the states of the Mexican union.

2

1871–1930

"There is no question in medicine that has been so debated as the question of provoked abortion." So observed physician Juan Breña in his defense of physicians' right—in fact, their duty—to perform surgical abortions on Mexican women. Performing such operations, Breña asserted, "is licit and fully justified . . . due to the indisputable importance and predominant role that women play in society and in the family." Breña did not present this position in 1974, or in 2007. He produced it in 1898, in a stirring defense of women's rights to surgical abortions published in the *Crónica médica Mexicana: Revista de medicina, cirugía y terapéutica y órgano de los hospitales de la república* (Mexican medical chronicle: review of medicine, surgery, and therapy and organ of the hospitals of the republic).[1]

Breña wrote his justification of surgical abortion in response to an article that another doctor, obstetrician Alberto López Hermosa, had published the previous year, taking the position that it was unethical and illicit for physicians to perform *abortos provocados*, which were abortions performed in the first six months of gestation, as opposed to *partos prematuros artificiales*, those performed in the final trimester of pregnancy, which he believed remained ethically sound and medically advantageous.[2] López Hermosa had called for the Mexican state to revise the articles of the Distrito Federal's 1871 penal code that treated abortion, asserting that the code should criminalize abortos provocados performed under any circumstances.

Breña vociferously championed the importance and legitimacy of therapeutic abortions, dismissing the implication that physicians in Mexico were in the habit of providing these to pregnant women without grave medical cause and congratulating his compatriots for their moral rectitude. Physicians and patients in Mexico City, he wrote, only sought or performed abortions where necessary and lawful, unlike in other international urban settings like Paris, London, and New York, where abortions had become routine, and where daily publications advertised "that this or that so-called SPECIALIST, who offers to remedy menstrual disorders and other feminine illnesses *guaranteeing* certain success, the innocuousness of the care, discretion, etc., etc."[3]

Breña also addressed the question of how to proceed if only the pregnant woman or the unborn product of conception could be saved. He said the choice was clear: women's lives should be privileged in these cases because of "their relations in society, their necessity within the family, the distinctions they have acquired . . . and their existence over many years." Only would theological precepts from ancient times accept the idea that "an unbaptized fetus, unpurged from original sin" should be valued more greatly than a woman.[4]

The conflict between these two turn-of-the-century physicians illuminates many of the issues with which this chapter is concerned. It focuses, first, on the specific nature of the 1871 criminal code, its diffusion in various parts of the Mexican republic, and its application by local and higher court justices in abortion trials. Second, it examines the broader social implications of the notable increase in the last decades of the nineteenth century of public denunciations of abortions and the relationship between this increase and shifting attitudes toward public morality in general and the sexuality of plebeian women in particular.

Finally, this chapter concludes with a discussion of the evidence that medical and medico-legal texts from the late nineteenth and early twentieth centuries contain about the participation of medical professionals in the performance of abortions. These sources reveal that while a faction of Mexico's medical establishment opposed the entire notion of professionally administered abortions, there were other practitioners, including Dr. Luis Hidalgo y Carpio, who advocated for its lawful practice under particular circumstances. Although the performance of surgical abortions may have been controversial, by 1900, if not earlier, the Escuela Nacional de Medicina listed the performance of them, along with embryotomies, as a requirement for those seeking qualification within the field of obstetrics.[5] In the first decades of the twentieth century, historian Beatriz Urías Horcasitas points out, it was not uncommon for medical reviews or theses to describe the necessity of performing surgical abortions.[6] Such evidence challenges many of our assumptions about the reasons for and roots of opposition to abortion in more recent periods.

Material in this chapter spans two periods in Mexican history normally presented as diametrically opposed to one another: the era of the Porfiriato (1876–1910), when Mexico was subjected to the modernizing authoritarian rule of Porfirio Díaz, and the revolutionary era (1910–40), when Mexico underwent a dramatic social, political, and cultural civil war, followed by a fifteen-year period in which the inheritors of the revolution established new laws, political parties, and social conventions that enshrined revolutionary society. Most histories understand Porfirian policies, which championed Mexico's modernization through the cultivation of foreign investment, facilitated the encroachment of large estate owners and railroad developers on small holder and community-held land, and that stifled political opposition, as the principal forces that provoked revolutionary resistance.[7] When it came, resistance to the Porfiriato was multifaceted and involved shifting alliances constructed between divergent groups: peasants, both rural and urban laborers, middle-class political dissidents, and powerful northern politicians and estate owners frustrated with their decades-long exclusion from the centers of political and economic power.

The political figures who seized power at the end of the revolution pivoted dramatically away from Porfirian cultural ideals (which had been oriented toward western Europe and especially France), and instituted dramatic changes in law and policy, expressed in such socialist objectives as the 1917 Constitution's support for workers' rights, land redistribution, and radical secularism. Eventually the revolutionary state also pursued state-supported programs in health care, education, and various forms of public assistance. However, scholars have also shown the myriad ways that the political party—the PRI—that emerged in the wake of the revolution and that became virtually synonymous with the federal government also reconstructed central elements of Porfirian rule in terms of both its longevity and its intolerance of political dissent.[8]

For women, the implications of the revolution were mixed. On the one hand, the devastating loss of life—by some estimates, as many as two million people died in the war—likely contributed to increased state and social pressure in the following generation that women's duty was to repopulate the country. Elizabeth O'Brien notes, for instance, that one medical student's 1933 thesis bemoaned the fact that rampant criminal abortions "threatened the growth and stability of the nation because Mexico had lost many to war and migration and because the vast territory needed to be (re)populated."[9] In the unbelievable view of this author, any woman who consented to sexual intercourse consented to reproduce. On the other, some of the rhetoric and some of the individual state leaders affiliated with the revolution supported feminist objectives: in 1919 the Mexican Feminist Council formed its wake, and the National Congress of Women Workers and Peasants held three conventions in the early 1930s. Scholars have recently examined the myriad ways that women helped transform Mexico during and after the revolution.[10] Despite the revolution's importance to Mexican women, and their contributions to its development, it is worth bearing in mind that despite the political and cultural distinctions historians often perceive between the Porfirian and revolutionary eras, very little about the country's medical, legal, or judicial practices relating to abortion changed between these two periods.

The Federal District's Penal Code of 1871

In 1871 the Federal District issued republican Mexico's first comprehensive penal code temporally disconnected from its political association with the liberal Constitution of 1857 by the War of Reforma (1857–62) and the Second Empire interregnum (1863–67). In 1870 President Benito Juárez appointed a federal commission, headed by minister of justice and public instruction Antonio Martínez de Castro, to complete the framing of the code first initiated in 1861. Martínez de Castro sought with this body of law to reform the convoluted colonial legal system that in his 1876 *Exposición de motivos del código penal* (Exposition on the motives for the penal code) he characterized as forged "in times of ignorance," dismissing the older system as designed for punitive rather than reformative outcomes and critiquing judicial personnel he characterized as arbitrary and capricious.[11] The Federal District's penal code of 1871 had only local jurisdiction over most crimes but national jurisdiction over those crimes (e.g., counterfeiting or contraband) enacted against the federal state. Modeled on examples from French, British, and other western European systems, the 1871 code aimed through its minute qualification of all possible extenuating and aggravating circumstances applicable in sentencing to mitigate against the discretionary powers of individual judges. Martínez de Castro also indicated that his commission had designed the new penal code with a view to encouraging the population to cooperate with the state to ensure that the public security of Mexican society "would be completely reestablished."[12]

Both because the new code included a significant departure from earlier legal treatments of abortion and because it had such an enduring influence on the subsequent legal treatment of abortion, it is worth discussing details of the new code in detail here. The author of the code's sections treating abortion was physician Luis Hidalgo y Carpio, an advocate of therapeutic abortions in cases where these were necessary.[13] Chapter 9, Article 569 of the 1871 Federal District's code defined abortion as "the extraction of the product of conception and its expulsion provoked by any means, no matter at what point in the pregnancy; in every case when this is done without necessity." The code distinguished fetal extraction or expulsion that occurred in the eighth month of pregnancy as "parto prematuro artificial" but indicated it should be penalized in the same way as abortion.[14] Other articles stated that an abortion was deemed necessary (and permissible) if a physician judged that pregnancy or birth posed the risk of death to the mother; declared the crime should only be punished only if it was completed (and not merely attempted); and announced that an abortion "caused only by the fault of the pregnant woman [in other words, accidental abortions caused by negligence] is not punishable."[15]

Much of the rest of the chapter focused on specifying the punishment for those convicted. Article 572 stated that medical personnel (doctors, surgeons, and midwives) convicted of the crime but who had provoked an abortion accidentally would be suspended from the exercise of their profession for one year. Article 579, however, declared that medical professionals who intentionally caused women to abort and, in so doing, ensured their deaths should be subject to the death penalty, or, in the case of attenuating circumstances, to ten years' imprisonment.

Under most circumstances a pregnant woman who procured an intentional abortion was to be punished with two years of imprisonment as long as she met with three qualifying circumstances: "1) That she was not of ill repute. 2) That she tried to hide her pregnancy. 3) That this was the fruit of an illegitimate union."[16] If either the first or second qualification were not met, the sentence would be increased by one year per condition; the absence of the third qualification implied an automatic total sentence of five years imprisonment, whatever the state of the other conditions. Later sections of chapter 9 declared that a person (apart from the pregnant woman herself) convicted of making a woman abort without "physical or moral violence" would serve four years in prison; those who used violence would serve six years.

The code's treatment of abortion contained several curious elements. Article 572 specified that only abortions classified as "grave" were punishable, without revealing what a non-grave abortion might constitute, although elsewhere the code suggested that individual judges could make such determinations.[17] Article 577 declared that sentences should be reduced by half "if the fetus was already dead" when the abortion was undertaken or if the procedure managed to save the life of the mother and child, both of which conditions appear to contradict the notion of "abortion." These articles were likely aimed at helping courts to judge cases of induced parto prematuro artificial. As Martínez de Castro explained elsewhere, "The seriousness of the crime diminishes greatly when the mother's life and the life of the child are saved." In such cases, he observed, the penalty should be reduced by half.[18]

Given its proximity to abortion, it is also instructive to examine the 1871 Federal District's treatment of infanticide, defined as the killing of an infant during the first seventy-two hours after birth. The code punished infanticide with less severity than homicide but sentenced those convicted to longer prison terms than those convicted of abortion. Prison terms were reduced if defendants met the same conditions respecting their public reputations as applied to abortion cases, with the additional clause that imprisonment might also be reduced if "the birth of the child had been hidden and had not been recorded in the civil registry," referring to the liberal state's 1859 requirement that all births, deaths, and marriages be publicly recorded in a state registry.[19]

Several elements of the 1871 code's treatment of reproductive crimes are worth highlighting. First, the code dramatically reduced the theoretical punishment for abortion, revising medieval and early modern notions that abortion and infanticide merited capital punishment in favor of terms of imprisonment for those guilty of either crime. Second (as we will discuss further), the 1871 code determined that abortions performed to save the pregnant woman's life were not punishable.[20] Contemporary physicians believed that various medical conditions might make abortions imperative. These included narrow pelvises, uterine tumors, uncontrollable vomiting or bleeding, retroversion of the uterus, eclampsia, and serious heart conditions.[21] Neither were punishable unintentional miscarriages that mothers provoked. Others who induced abortions unintentionally (as Hidalgo y Carpio and Dr. Gustavo Ruiz y Sandoval, his coauthor of a foundational medico-legal text, explained elsewhere), by inviting pregnant women to engage in inappropriately vigorous dancing, by shooting off firearms near them, or by requiring them to take long walks or horseback rides, should also be treated with greater leniency.[22]

Finally, the 1871 code privileged the defense of honor as legitimate grounds to reduce the severity of sentences for those convicted. Martínez de Castro extended the same consideration to the sentencing of mothers for the crime of infanticide as for abortion, observing that "no modern legislation punishes infanticide with the death penalty when a mother commits the crime to hide her dishonor."[23] The novelty of honor's articulation in the code lay in both its precise reasoning about those cases in which defendants' sentences should be lightened to protect individual, familial, and community honor, and in its explicit connections to the maintenance of public order, expressed in the Porfirian state's vigorous campaigns to encourage population size, improve hygiene, preserve public order, and impose limitation on vices and luxury.[24]

Scholars see the centrality of honor in both judicial and medical perceptions of abortion in this era and long after it.[25] Saydi Núñez Cetina comments that the social mandate to prioritize the protection of female sexual honor, familial respectability, and legitimacy for the purposes of inheritance all endured into the mid-twentieth century, despite some of the significant societal changes the postrevolutionary state adopted. Between 1914 and 1931, the Mexican state passed a variety of measures that supported the notion of women's equality to men, including the legalization of divorce, salary equalization, the establishment of women's rights to independent legal and judicial rights, and equal rights over children's custody.[26] Despite these initiatives, however, in the postrevolutionary era, as before it, for judges assessing guilt and innocence in abortion and infanticide cases, "notions of honor and legitimacy weighed more than the protection of the lives and integrity of infants."[27] Indeed, the imperative to preserve familial honor and police women's sexual virtue was sufficiently pronounced in the late nineteenth century that domestic violence was both common and judicially condoned as an imperative for men required to correct the sexual or social misbehavior of women in their households.[28]

Details of the 1871 code treating abortion are crucial not only because they affected how justices ruled on these crimes in the eras of the Porfiriato and the revolution but also because many of them were maintained in subsequent criminal codes throughout the twentieth century. Within five years of 1871, many other states in the republic had issued their own criminal codes, often adopting the Federal District's version with few modifications. The state of Oaxaca was somewhat exceptional: it passed its own penal code in 1870, which it had begun developing in 1850. The Oaxaca code's discussion of abortion differed slightly from the 1871 code. Oaxaca offered fewer protections to pregnant women who either needed to end pregnancies for health reasons or who unintentionally miscarried, decreeing that voluntary abortion, whether by "drinks, blows, or any other means," and whether induced by the mother or another person, would be punished with the same severity as voluntary homicide—that is to say, with between six and twenty years' imprisonment, although prison terms would be halved if the abortion transpired in the first trimester of pregnancy. If a pregnant woman caused an abortion by negligence, she would be fined between ten and one hundred pesos (convertible to one day of imprisonment for every half peso).[29] Oaxaca's code made no mention of the reduction of sentences in cases where the preservation of women's honor was at stake. Although on paper, then, Oaxaca seemed to treat abortion more harshly than did other parts of the country, in practice the few abortion trials preserved from this state in the decades after 1870 do not show justices ruling more harshly in trials there than elsewhere.

Many other states treated abortion identically or nearly identically to the Federal District. Puebla, for instance, adopted the district's code in 1875 and modified nothing in its chapter treating abortion.[30] Sonora did the same, although it published its state code later, in 1884. Yucatán adopted the Distrito Federal code in 1872, modifying the chapters only by slightly reducing the length of imprisonment for the convicted.[31] Tlaxcala adopted the 1871 code in 1879 with minor changes, including the omission of the one-year suspension from practice for medical personnel convicted of performing or providing abortions, reducing the length of imprisonment sentences, and omitting the possibility of capital punishment for convicted medical professionals.[32] Thus we have a clear idea of how the law theoretically treated those suspected of abortion. But what happened in practice?

Abortion Trials, 1871–1930

The set of judicial cases discussed in the following section come largely from the holdings of three state judicial archives, those of Oaxaca, Yucatán, and Tlaxcala (table 1).[33] This discussion does not include the many cases of accidental abortions (apparently unintentional miscarriages) that these collections contain because they do not document attitudes and practices concerning abortion as reproductive control. Nor does this discussion include the dozens of cases that record fetal corpses that members of the public encountered in public and reported to judicial authorities, but about which no further evidence surfaced to allow courts to pursue their investigations.

In the group of cases studied here, the parties held responsible for terminating pregnancies were almost always pregnant women, as was also true for cases involving infanticide. Of hundreds of Mexican infanticide and abortion trials spanning from the seventeenth to the twentieth centuries, in only one case did a legal official suggest that the man who had impregnated a woman under investigation should also bear some criminal responsibility for ending a pregnancy or a newborn life. This occurred in the 1865 trial of Ynes Euan, an Indigenous woman who worked as a domestic servant in Campeche, Yucatán. Euan's legal defender argued that the son of the owner of the house in which she worked, who had "seduced" her, should be under criminal investigation rather than his client. The fiscal in Mérida's superior court concurred and asserted that Euan's seducer should be under investigation for the crime of *estupro*.[34] As Reuben Zahler comments in his examination of infanticide trials in early republican Venezuela, "[The] unwillingness to even identity the father indicates a desire on the part of judicial officials to discount men from 'reproductive responsibility.'"[35]

As table 1 illustrates, a much larger body of abortion trials exists in the collection of the Tribunal Superior de Justicia del Distrito Federal (TSJDF), a court the 1857 Constitution created as the appellate court of the Distrito Federal. However, this archive is organized only by year, and while a catalog list of the entire series indicates the subject of each case, six weeks of searching uncovered only two cases from within the group of indicated trials for aborto (although many more for *infanticidio* cases). Although some of the cases in this collection no doubt include unintentional miscarriages as well as intentional abortions, the total body of TSJDF cases listed in the catalog indicates that a dramatic increase occurred in investigations for abortions in the decades after 1870, particularly in the 1880s and the 1920s.

Taken together, both the trials housed in state-level judicial archives shown in table 1 and those from the TSJDF series shown in table 2 demonstrate that a significant increase in the number of abortion cases Mexican courts tried in the six decades after 1871 in comparison to the five decades before it. Whereas this same set of archives turned up only ten abortion trials in the first half-century after independence, in the sixty years after 1871 there were a total of 247 cases. Statistics published by the Mexican state in the period between 1892 and 1905 in the *Cuadros estadísticos e informe del procurador de Justicia* (Statistical tables and report by the attorney general) also document a large number of aborto cases tried within this period: 193.[36] The increase is also evident, given the fact that the state judicial archives of Oaxaca, Yucatán, and Tlaxcala include both the viceregal and early postindependence collections, and courts tried a paucity of abortion cases in these decades.[37]

Along with archival evidence, increased reports of aborted fetuses found in public spaces are also evident in news sources from the last decades of the century. The policing notes of one capital city newspaper, *El Republicano*, recorded on May 31, 1874, that "Felipa was pregnant, procured an abortion and then threw the fetus in the rubbish dump," and that "the cadaver of a new born girl was found by the sexton of [the church of] Santo Domingo, wrapped in some newspapers."[38] *La Libertad*, the house organ of the Porfirian state, reported on August 6, 1878, that another woman, "before her period of gestation was concluded, wished for her fetus to see the light of day." The paper charged she had taken steps to prematurely birth her baby, and for this reason, she was interviewed by the police.[39] The capital's biweekly paper, *La Orquesta*, reported on June 3, 1871, that "a heinous abomination of nature that can only outrageously be called a mother, incomprehensibly resolved to throw the fruit of her womb in the masonry (*albañil*) of house no. 10 of the Jesús María Street. This case has no explanation. It almost has no name."[40] News stories such as these lambasted women who disposed of their newborns as monstrous and unfathomable.

Denunciations for the crime of abortion showed a marked increase in the decades after 1870, although the rise in numbers of these cases was much smaller than the increase in the numbers of infanticide denunciations in the same period. The sections of the consulted state judicial archives for Tlaxcala, Yucatán, and Oaxaca (as well as the municipal archives of Oaxaca City) between 1871 and 1930 contain a total of 133 infanticide trials.[41] The TSJDF series in the National Archives houses an additional 80 infanticide cases for the period from 1871 to 1899 alone. Although they reflected similar circumstances and often similar motivations, infanticide was much more commonly denounced and investigated than was abortion.

Abortion was a more secretive crime than infanticide. As Luis Hidalgo y Carpio commented in his 1877 tract, *Compendio de medicina legal* (Digest of legal medicine), it was impossible to pinpoint the frequency with which women aborted their fetuses in Mexico because abortion was a crime "that is committed with great discretion and can be hidden better from the vigilant eye of the police."[42] Pregnant women had recourse to medicinal means of provoking abortions more easily and effectively in the first months of pregnancy, a period during which their pregnancies might not have visually registered with other members of their communities, and when the product of conception had not developed sufficiently to necessarily present incriminating evidence if its development was interrupted. Finally, as in the colonial era, natural or unintentional miscarriages were so common that it was hard for anyone to determine when the interruption of pregnancy had been accidental or intentional.

To summarize: between 1871 and 1930, Mexican women sought to limit reproduction through abortion, among other means, and courts increasingly prosecuted them for this act, even though in this period abortion remained a crime that was much less frequently prosecuted than the related crimes of infanticide or abandonment. This evidence challenges Fernanda Núñez Becerra's argument that the paucity of judicial records involving abortion dating from this period indicates that, prior to the twentieth century, Mexican women did not possess a "contraceptive mentality" such as did their contemporaries in France, England, the United States, and Canada who actively sought abortions to limit childbirth.[43] One of the statistics that Núñez Becerra uses to support her assertion of the absence of contraceptive practices among Mexican women was their alleged high fecundity rate of 178.53 births per 1,000 women in 1900

Table 1. Abortion trials (Oaxaca, Yucatán, Tlaxcala, Distrito Federal), 1871–1930

YEAR	PLACE	REFERENCE	DEFENDANT	SENTENCE
1875	Mérida, Yuc.	AGEY, Justicia, Penal, caja 172, vol. 172, exp. 65	María Dolores Herrera	Acquitted
1875	Teposcolula, Oax.	AHJO, Teposcolula, Criminal, caja 107, exp. 27	Ana Vázquez	Acquitted
1879	Villa Alta, Oax.	AHJO, Villa Alta, Criminal, legajo 108, exp. 3	Josefina Sebastiana	Acquitted
1880	Villa Alta, Oax.	AHJO, Villa Alta, Criminal, legajo 109, exp. 3	María Jimenes	Acquitted
1883	Oaxaca City, Oax.	AHMO, Justicia, Juzgado, 10 criminal, subseries: procesos, caja 24	Juana López	Acquitted
1883	Mexico City	AGNM, TSJDF 1883, caja 841	Pomposa Acosta	Released in "conditional liberty"
1884	Oaxaca City, Oax.	AHMO, Justicia, Corte de Justicia, 1a sala, 1883–84, caja 7	María Reyes and María Anacleta	Acquitted
1889	Villa Alta, Oax.	AHJO, Villa Alta, Criminal, caja 125, exp. 6	Paula Gernónimo Zelaá	Acquitted
1890	Villa Alta, Oax.	AHJO, Villa Alta, Criminal, caja 127, exp. 30	Isabel Diego Ysidros	Acquitted
1890	Huajuapan, Oax.	AHJO, Huajuapan, Criminal, caja 263, exp. 26		Not pursued
1894	Aytec, Tlax.	AHET, Justicia, Criminal, caja 338, exp. 25	Eduviges Ramírez	Acquitted
1896	Mérida, Yuc.	AGEY, Justicia, Penal, vol. 62, exp. 29	Maximiliana Osorio	Not pursued

Year	Location	Source	Name	Outcome
1896	Mérida, Yuc.	AGEY, Justicia, Penal, vol. 69, exp. 48	Mercedes Gonzales	Not pursued
1899	Mérida, Yuc.	AGEY, Justicia, Penal, vol. 132, exp. 34; vol. 139, exp. 28	Fernanda and Norberta Canche	Acquitted (of abortion charge)
1902	Mérida, Yuc.	AGEY, Justicia, Penal, caja 517, vol. 13, exp. 4	Rudesindo May	Acquitted
1902	Mérida, Yuc.	AGEY, Justicia, Penal, caja 529, vol. 25, exp. 20	Hilario Poot	Not pursued
1902	Huamantla, Tlax.	AHET, Justicia, Criminal, caja 376, exp. 17	Eulalia Aguilar	Convicted (1 year, 3 months imprisonment)
1904	Mérida, Yuc.	AGEY, Justicia, Penal, caja 588, vol. 84, exp. 28	María Medina	Acquitted
1906	Mérida, Yuc.	AGEY, Justicia, Penal, caja 618, vol. 114, exp. 25	María Remedios Teh	Acquitted
1909	Mérida, Yuc.	AGEY, Justicia, Penal, caja 712, vol. 66, exp. 50	Timotea May	Defendant died before verdict issued

Source: Created by the author from the AGEY, AHJO, AHMO, TSJDF, AHET Judicial Archives.

Table 2. Abortion cases cataloged in the Fondo Tribunal Superior de Justicia del Distrito Federal (TSJDF), by decade, 1871–1930

DECADE	NUMBER OF CASES
1871–1880	2
1881–1890	57
1891–1900	23
1901–1910	22
1911–1920	19
1921–1929	104
Total	227

Source: Created by the author from the TSJDF catalog.

in comparison to contemporaneous France, and present-day Mexico City, both of which have rates of about 22 births per 1,000 women.[44] However, other scholars have questioned the accuracy of this very high fecundity rate, which was based on Porfirian statistics. In fact there is considerable evidence that a more accurate fecundity rate for Mexican women in 1900 would be much lower, between 50 and 54 births per 1,000 women.[45]

Whether by abortion or contraception, the question of Mexican women's successful control over their fertility in the nineteenth century merits reexamination. Criminal cases are useful for establishing both community concerns and judicial reasoning about crime but are not always explicit about defendants' motives and methods. Many of the trials examined here do not contain detailed information about the means by which women allegedly aborted, nor do they provide a great deal of biographical details about these figures. From those cases where such information is recorded, we learn that almost all defendants in abortion cases were the pregnant women themselves, although in two cases courts investigated mothers of these women for supplying their daughters with abortifacients. Most defendants charged were unmarried and young (in their twenties or under twenty years old). Most of them were from the "popular classes," but at least one, Pomposa Acosta, was a woman of means.[46] Several were Indigenous and required court translators. One was a native of Valencia, Spain. An additional 1925 abortion case is not included in the database because its dossier has not been located. However, a summary of the trial reprinted in the *Periódico Oficial* of the state of Chiahuahua reported that that state had reinstated the right of a physician, Conrad von Shoech, to practice medicine in the capital after having revoked it one year earlier "because he had been tried for the crime of forced abortion." A state supreme court judge had absolved him of the crime.[47]

Women investigated for committing abortion in this era most often had allegedly ingested a substance to induce a preterm miscarriage, although, in one case, asphyxiation was the cause of fetal death. Defendants or other witnesses in abortion cases asserted that pregnant women had ingested unspecified drinks. For example, a first-instance court in Mérida initiated an investigation into Mercedes Gonzales's abortion in 1896, when an official from the city's Hospital O'Horán informed the court that Gonzales had appeared at the institution two days earlier and told the presiding physician that someone "had administered medicines to her that had made her abort."[48] Under interrogation Gonzales denied this and declared that a fright had provoked her miscarriage, and that two midwives attending her shortly thereafter had subsequently delivered "a mass" that "had absolutely no human form."[49] In Fernanda and Norberta Canche's 1899 trial, the court investigated both women for supplying Fernanda's young daughter with an abortifacient medicine, identified as a drink of "the leaves of verbena," a flowering plant used to treat *pasmo* (amenorrhea).[50] In a 1902 trial from Huamantla, Tlaxcala, the accused declared she had miscarried after having drunk a "purgative of powders of Jalapa."[51] There is some evidence that midwives or other medical personnel provided women with surgical or physical abortions in this era as well. One Mexico City newspaper account from 1895 described a landlady who, for a fee, aided her tenants to "procure and provoke abortions by any means."[52] A 1907 newspaper article recounted how one Mexico City physician, Dr. Rees, had been imprisoned in the Belén penitentiary, accused of provoking the death of a patient with an operation he performed that provoked an abortion.[53] A 1925 abortion trial before the TSJDF involved a midwife, Beatriz Mejía Sánchez, alleged to have induced an abortion in a young woman who died from an infection contracted after the incomplete extraction of an embryo.[54]

Beyond court records medical and medico-legal tracts provide other information about contemporary methods to induce or execute abortions. Physician Luis Hidalgo y Carpio asserted in his *Compendio de medicina legal* in 1877 that women who sought to abort "have frequently used abundant bleedings," draining blood from either the arm or ankle, or applying leeches to the area around the vulva. All the examples Hidalgo y Carpio cited, like almost all the abortifacient medicines he discussed, including *sabina* (juniper), *ruda* (rue), *cuernecillo de centeno* (ergot), and *sulfato de quinina* (quinine sulfate), may have been used in Mexico, but were derived from evidence taken from European tracts.[55]

Other late nineteenth-century sources also indicate that women continued to use cihuapatli and other labor accelerators dating from the pre-Columbian period as abortifacients at the turn of the twentieth century. Physician Fernando Altamirano, who published his medical thesis on the therapeutic properties of plants indigenous to Mexico in an 1877 edition of the science periodical *La Naturaleza*, noted that the flowers of *chamolxochitl* (*Laennecia filaginoides*), a plant common to much of central-south Mexico, could provoke an abortion.[56] One late nineteenth-century physician in his article on the performance of embryotomies began by commenting that a frequent cause of *distocia* (difficult or obstructed labor) was women's inappropriate consumption of cihuapatli, "a very well-known herb by people in our poorer classes, and which, without any restriction at all, circulates in the streets and markets where it is sold by those ambulatory sellers called *herbolarios* [herb vendors]."[57] Further, he commented, not only did the illiterate classes use the plant to stimulate contractions, but also "some doctors recommend and prescribe it regularly in their practices in all circumstances."[58]

An 1880 investigation by a commission of the Superior Board of Health, published in the daily paper *El Siglo Diez y Nueve*, reported that it was widely known that within the Volador market in Mexico City there was an herb stall selling many plants of questionable purpose. In secrecy the commissioners purchased various plants from it, including *cihuapatli, marihuana, falsa belladonna, toloachi* (nightshade; *Datura innoxia*), *codos de fraile* (yellow oleander seeds), and *yerba de la Puebla* (*Senecio canicida*). "As is clear," they concluded, "anybody can obtain with the greatest ease an abortive or any other plant of those reputed to highly poisonous."[59] And a 1892 investigation into a possible abortion a woman had undertaken prior to her admission to Mexico City's Maternity Hospital, the Casa de Maternidad, described how the casa's head midwife declared she had been unable to extract the product of conception from the woman's uterus after the cihuapatli she had taken had produced an infection in her womb.[60] Public health officials investigating high rates of maternal mortality at the casa in the 1880s also disparaged Mexican women's ongoing practices of using such remedies, which they said endangered women's health.[61]

Some contemporary infanticide cases contain further details about other abortifacient concoctions women used at the turn of the century. In 1903 two neighbors denounced Escolástica Alcocer to a tribunal in Mérida, describing how they had seen her mother and brother burying a newborn corpse one night. Other witnesses testified that Alcocer's mother had asked for several abortive "potions" from a pharmacist.[62] Shortly thereafter José Jesús Cervesa, a mechanic who said he possessed a certain amount of botanical knowledge, appeared before the court and declared that Alcocer and her mother had consulted with him for a cure because the former had ceased to menstruate. He had supplied Alcocer with a medicine composed of saffron and *semen contra*.[63] The latter was the common name for altamisa, a plant discussed in chapter 1 that women had used for centuries to induce miscarriages.[64]

One salient feature in the body of abortion trials in this era was their high acquittal rate.[65] Of the twenty complete cases located, only one ended in a guilty conviction: the 1902 trial of Eulalia Aguilar in Huamantla, Tlaxcala, who had confessed to procuring an abortion by asking her mother "to give her a purge made from the powders of Jalapa," which, "according to expert testimony, sufficed to produce this effect."[66] Although Aguilar later retracted this confession and said her arduous work collecting firewood and water had caused her to miscarry accidentally, her judges deemed her initial confession sufficient grounds to convict her to one year, three months, and fifteen days imprisonment. Judges were reluctant to convict in abortion cases without indisputable evidence, and given the private nature of the crime, the only form this was likely to take was the defendant's confession. Although, in this matter, Aguilar's judges ruled consistently with the decrees of Tlaxcala's penal code, their judgment was inconsistent with the code in one sense. Tlaxcala's code, like most others, declared that, apart from the pregnant woman, those who, apparently like Aguilar's mother, "without physical or moral violence makes a woman abort" should be sentenced to between three and four years' imprisonment.[67] Yet, although the court determined Aguilar's mother had supplied her with an effective abortifacient, it made no move to convict her.

In the 1883 Mexico City trial of Pomposa Acosta, the court did focus its attention on the mother of a young woman, Elvira Prieto. After impregnating and then abandoning her, Prieto's estranged lover accused Pomposa Acosta of supplying her daughter with an abortifacient. In this case, however, Prieto denied having consumed (or even requesting) the substance, so the court placed Acosta in "provisional liberty" without specifying what this entailed. Acosta's legal defender requested her full liberty, because, he argued, her ongoing allegation of guilt was harming her honor and reputation, but the case file ends without a record of the final outcome of this appeal.[68]

Judges did not normally convict defendants, for several reasons. They often found evidence for conviction lacking, given the lack of eyewitnesses. They also ascertained that there were many other plausible explanations that could explain the cause of an unintentional miscarriage, which made it hard to be certain that the abortion had been intentional. One contemporary source, the 1868 *Estudio sobre el aborto* (Study of miscarriage), listed various behaviors that might cause spontaneous abortion: weak constitutions, illness, violent sports, tight dresses, sewing with a pedal machine, and having sexual relations while pregnant.[69] As several historians have suggested, it may also be the case that judges treated unmarried, impoverished, and, frequently, Indigenous women accused of reproductive crimes with particular leniency both because of a paternalistic notion that they should grant special indulgence to less powerful members of society, and because of their support for the Porfirian state's promotion of the importance of privileging the discourses of familial honor and social stability above all other considerations.[70]

In these abortion cases, with the exception of Eulalia Aguilar's subsequently retracted confession, defendants generally denied having intentionally aborted, so their trials do not contain discussions of defendants' views on whether the imperative to defend their sexual honor motivated their actions. In contemporary infanticide trials, however, defendants occasionally did confess to their crimes and often asserted that the desire to preserve their reputations in the community or their fear of the anger their pregnancies and births would provoke in other family members had prompted them to act. Guadalupe Martínez, tried for infanticide in Teposcolula, Oaxaca, in 1875 after townspeople uncovered the body of her newborn, which she had abandoned near a pile of rocks in a public square, told the court she had given birth secretly because she was fearful of punishment from her parents or her uncle.[71] And in her 1895 infanticide trial, Victoria Zapata, of Maxcanú, Yucatán, confessed that she had hidden her pregnancy and the (stillborn) birth of her child "because of the excessive fear she had of her father because he is severe in punishing her and she feared he would mistreat her."[72] In these cases the defense of honor remained at the foundation of defendants' actions because the loss of familial honor was what defendants feared would prompt the outrage of paternal outrage and violence.

Scrutinizing the Female Sex

Community members initiated abortion (and infanticide) trials by denouncing their peers to local courts in the decades after 1871 either due to their knowledge about the crimes they derived from the relevant sections of the 1871 penal code or, as seems more likely, independently of such an awareness. Either way the rising numbers of cases brought before magistrates makes clear that Mexicans intensified their scrutiny of female peers' reproductive practice in the closing decades of the nineteenth century. Who engaged in this scrutiny, and why did it happen? Parties who initially denounced women for abortion are unrecorded in just under half of the existent abortion cases. Of the remaining cases, family members of pregnant women initiated the cases six times, neighbors three times, and once each by an estranged lover and a medical official. Let us take a closer look.

In the town of Villa Hidalgo, Oaxaca, in 1880 an alcalde opened an investigation after "public rumor" prompted him to question Indigenous resident María Jiménez, who had given birth but not baptized her baby, allegedly because she had killed it.[73] Court officials found Jiménez in bed at home, bleeding, a condition she said she had caused when she "gave herself a blow falling on the ground." Two midwives who examined Jiménez supported this interpretation of her injuries. However, one of Jiménez's neighbors, forty-five-year-old Victoriano Mendez (the likely originator of the public rumor), declared he had observed that Jiménez was pregnant one month earlier but later noted that she no longer carried the child. He also claimed he had heard the cry of a newborn criatura one night.[74] Another neighbor, presumably the wife of Mendez, confirmed his testimony. However, in a careo (face-to-face reconciliation between witnesses whose testimony differed), Jiménez explained that conflicts about other matters had provoked the denunciation. As she put it, "Her neighbor got angry over matters concerning neighbors—land, [raising] roosters, [raising] hens—that bothered both of them."[75] The court determined there was no foundation to the rumors of her pregnancy or abortion and acquitted Jiménez. In this case Mendez may not have primarily had concerns about his neighbor's reproductive practices, but the fact that such concerns registered with him as a possible strategy for attacking his neighbor is nonetheless significant.

In other trials family members of women who had either aborted or miscarried came forward to register the circumstances of what they described as unintentional miscarriages to local criminal courts to preempt the possibility of more malicious inquiries into their relatives' experiences. In 1875 in the small community of San Pedro Topiltepec within the district of Teposcolula, Oaxaca, a day laborer, Toribio Vázquez, appeared before a first-instance judge to inform him that he had seen a criatura laid out dead on the table belonging to his sister, Ana Vázquez, the previous day.[76] Toribio Vázquez declared that he did not suspect his sister, identified as "of Indigenous Mexican race," aged thirty-five, of provoking an abortion, because "she has no motive to do it since she is free and lives alone in her house without fear."[77] Nevertheless he felt compelled to register the misbirth with the court. Ana Vázquez, when she appeared, reiterated her brother's view, declaring she had no motivation to provoke an abortion "since she is not married, does not live with anybody and does not have anyone to fear and in addition is not a first-time mother so that neither for shame nor for any other motive could anything be suspected of her."[78] Interestingly, the siblings displayed here how members of their small, primarily Indigenous community reconciled their own views to the idea of the primacy of female sexual honor articulated in the 1871 penal code's pronouncements about honor and abortion. While registering that they recognized that women impregnated extra- or premaritally might have had a motivation to abort their fetuses to preserve public honor, Toribio and Ana both asserted that since Ana was neither married nor a known virgin, she had no honor to lose. In her case the absence of sexual honor actually worked to protect her judicially, supporting the position that she lacked a motivation to commit abortion.

In a second case from a small community in Villa Alta, Oaxaca, a woman appeared before a local judge to register that her daughter had accidentally miscarried a fetus after having carried water home from the town's well. The court accepted her explanation and did not pursue the case beyond a physical examination of the pregnant woman.[79] A mother opened a similar case about her daughter in the town of Lachirioag, Oaxaca, in June 1890.[80] Although in none of these cases did family members appear to have malicious intent in reporting misbirths, they do suggest that Mexicans during this time were aware that either neighbors or state officials were monitoring women's pregnancies and their outcomes. Tranquilina Poot of the small community of Mama, Yucatán, made this concern explicit when she informed the court in 1902 that her daughter had miscarried a fetus earlier that day, when she gave birth one month prematurely: "She pleaded that the authorities should examine the criatura and the mother because it is possible that it might be thought that her daughter hurt or killed the criatura she miscarried."[81]

Family members also initiated cases intending to harm those they denounced. In one trial a man denounced Pomposa Acosta as the interfering mother of his estranged lover who had induced an abortion in her daughter.[82] In Paula Gerónimo Zelaá's 1889 trial in Villa Hidalgo, the defendant's former mother-in-law accused her of aborting an extramarital pregnancy, an act Gerónimo Zelaá vigorously denied.[83] Two midwives testified that the defendant showed signs of a recent pregnancy and birth and noted that her breasts were full of milk. Despite this physical evidence, as well as the first-instance court's ruling that the defendant be placed in a recogimiento, the state supreme court overturned the lower court's ruling and, referring to a technicality in the *Código de Procedimientos Criminales* (Code of criminal law procedures), declared that the defendant should be freed.[84] Another case, reported in Mexico City's daily newspaper *La Patria* in 1897, described how a young employee of the Casa Amiga de la Obrera, a school for the children of working mothers, had been impregnated by another casa worker and had taken "a liquid" to provoke a miscarriage. The newspaper admonished that such promiscuity was frequent among both sexes in the service of both public and private businesses.[85]

The increase in public denunciations of both abortion and infanticide cases shows that the public's enthusiasm for policing women's sexual and reproductive practices increased in this era, or at least their acceptance of the obligation to police it rose. This was visibly true in cases of lower-class women who constituted the defendants in these cases. But why? Several explanations are possible. First, the Mexican liberal state, like its peers across Latin America, vigorously adopted the notion that endless expansion of the population was in the economic best interest of the country. In such a context, as Silvia Federici reminds us, resonated in earlier periods in Europe, any time population growth "became a major social concern . . . heresy became associated with reproductive crimes, especially 'sodomy,' infanticide, and abortion."[86] The policing of female sexuality might reflect the population's absorption of liberal and Porfirian efforts to control and sanitize plebeian populations, enacted in such measures as the regulation of prostitution, and as part of the general effort to encourage socially desirable gendered behavior, such as virtuous motherhood, modesty, and feminine dependency.[87] Elisa Speckman observes that Porfirian criminologists idealized traits in women they characterized as essentially feminine (passivity, self-control, docility, and submission), and that they feared that transgressions of any portion of this ideal could quickly spiral into women's participation in more extreme transgressions and crimes.[88] In just this period, middle-class women were challenging traditional domestic gender roles in their initial movement into professional educational programs, employment, and feminist publications.[89] Furthermore, damage to a woman's reputation was also taken seriously because it reflected badly on the status of male family members, and on men's public reputations as orderly rulers of their homes. In the context of the enormous rise in both female rural to urban migration and women's entry into the workforce outside of domestic service that characterized this era, the public, meanwhile, may have been especially zealous in its scrutiny of female propriety.[90]

In the context of the social and economic transformations of the Porfiriato, Laura Shelton, who studies the state of Sonora, also suggests another explanation for why members of the public more frequently denounced reproductive crimes to criminal courts. Shelton writes that the plebeian men who most often denounced members of their communities for abortion or infanticide between 1855 and 1910 possessed the same ideas about female sexual conduct as did Porfirian criminologists partially because of the "displacements associated with the accelerating rhythm of new life at the local level and the changes that undermined traditional masculinity fundamentally those relating to the possession of land, political autonomy, and men's position at the head of family networks."[91] In other words, a crisis of the diminishment of the traditional arenas of masculine authority provoked men to assert patriarchal authority in one of the few venues that remained available to them: scrutinizing women in their localities. Shelton additionally sees this tendency reflected in the contemporaneous rise of production of moralistic literature in popular presses and newspapers about the menace of moral and sexual degradation in this era of rapid change. She observes, too, that in this period, physicians were fundamentally unable to perceive the physiological signs on their patients between an induced abortion and an accidental miscarriage, and so, following the advice of forensic scientific manuals, physicians and judges alike were likely to try securing such insight by questioning women's peers and family members.[92]

If community members, in the closing decades of the nineteenth century, were more prone to denouncing women for reproductive crimes, contemporary documents indicate that the state also augmented its scrutiny in this era. In the context of the campaign to centrally register prostitutes in the face of the rise of syphilis outbreaks in the mid-1860s, the *Gaceta médica de México* reported in an article in 1863 that a division of the Mexican Army stationed in Michoacán had demanded that the principal surgeon of the region examine all members of the regiment and report on whether or not they were infected by venereal disease. The physicians indicated their qualms about how such reporting would compromise medical confidentiality. The *Gaceta*'s editors addressed the issue by reviewing physicians' legal obligations to report to the state on the conditions of their patients. These included, as set out in a federal law of November 1, 1865, the obligation that "all professors of medicine and surgery, who, in examining a patient become suspicious that a criminal event has occurred, whether an abortion or any other violent act, are obliged to give an account of this to the judicial authorities, so these may proceed to investigate the crime." Hidalgo y Carpio, the article's author, strenuously objected to this requirement, declaring that doctors were required to comply with the law, "but not with the unjust laws."[93] As discussed in this chapter's closing section, it is clear that a certain sector of the medical community not only resisted reporting criminal abortions to the state but also participated in performing what they viewed as licit abortions, even when other sectors of their profession considered these immoral if not illegal.

It would be reasonable to assume that two other factors might have provoked a rise in denunciations of both abortion and infanticide in the period after 1870. First, we might consider whether the augmentation of social concerns over the welfare, value, and innate human rights of unborn fetuses or newborn infants might have been responsible for the change. Did the population, the state, or the medical sector take up the defense of the fetus, as happened at the close of the twentieth century? Apparently not. For all their articulation of the importance of the family and the virtues of motherhood, Porfirian *científicos* advanced no programs, beyond hosting the Primer Congreso Higiénico Pedagógico (First Pedagogical Hygiene Congress) in Mexico City in 1882, that strove to address the medical, social, and economic realities of impoverished infants and children.

In her examination of children's welfare in Porfirian and revolutionary Mexico, Ann Blum observes that early twentieth-century state officials voiced a perspective of the rights and abilities of young children that was largely devoid of compassion. One official famously commented that abandoned children seven years or older could provide for their own subsistence and so did not require state assistance.[94] And while the Porfirian press may have bemoaned the astoundingly high rates of infant mortality—nationally three hundred deaths per thousand live births from the 1890s through 1910—the state's economic and social policies exacerbated rather than alleviated the death toll.[95]

Some evidence of changes in terms of state attitudes toward the welfare of children occurred in the early postrevolutionary era. These included the 1917 Constitution's protections against child labor; the hosting of the Primer Congreso Mexicano del Niño (First Mexican Congress on the Child), initiated in 1920; and the 1923 foundation of the *casas del pueblo* (rural schools), which subsequently became Mexico's broad system of rural schools.[96] However, none of these measures translated to the creation of a broad public discourse championing the inherent legal rights of newborns or fetuses. Nor did they affect judicial rulings on abortion through the 1920s, which continued to prioritize the importance of the defense of female honor over the notion of the inherent value of fetal or newborn life.[97]

We should also consider whether changing Catholic sensibilities over the centuries-old question of the moment that God endowed a developing human egg with a soul provoked an increased sensitivity to policing abortion after 1871. Did widely held religious ideas about the value of human lives at the moment of conception change in this period? Surviving evidence does not support this idea either. None of the parties involved in the abortion trials examined in this chapter referred to the soul, or to the human value of aborted fetuses. No discussion of the topic appeared in any searching of the late nineteenth-century sermons examined, nor in the ecclesiastical regulations passed by the Fourth Mexican Council that met in 1896, nor in Mexican catechisms published in this era, although matters pertaining to abortion did continue to circulate in confessional texts published in earlier periods. Elizabeth O'Brien has recently argued that Mexico's eighteenth-century priesthood and nineteenth-century medical profession championed the idea of fetal personhood in their commission of what she calls "sacred surgery," caesarean sections undertaken to ensure salvation through baptism of fetuses extracted from dead mothers' wombs.[98] Still, this does not seem to have been a set of beliefs or that either priests or physicians successfully transmitted to large sectors of the Mexican population, who often resisted the procedure.

While the papacy did issue two late nineteenth-century pronouncements directly or indirectly condemning abortion—*Apostolicae Sedis* (1869) and *Arcanum Divinae* (1880), which promoted the sanctity of marriage—as discussed earlier, neither pronouncement generated dramatic local responses within Mexico. When they did discuss the issue of abortion, rather than adopting a unilateral position, late nineteenth-century Catholic sources present a complex portrait of the question of the inherent value of unborn fetuses and the ethics of abortion. The *Diccionario de ciencias eclesiásticas* (Dictionary of ecclesiastical sciences), a theological compilation composed under the advisement of Spain's ecclesiastical hierarchy, contains extensive discussions about abortion and the status of *abortos* and *abortivos* (aborted entities). The *Diccionario* condemned abortion, asserting the Catholic Church had always viewed the act with horror and insisting that the human soul existed from the first moments of conception, a position it decreed essential to acceptance of the newly established doctrine of the Immaculate Conception.[99] But the text also acknowledged that the inherent legal rights of abortivos were nonexistent.

To avoid being classified as an abortivo, newborns had to be born alive, live for more than twenty-four hours after birth, be baptized before dying, and "be born at a stage where it can live naturally"—that is, at least at six months' gestation. Abortivos, those who did not meet all four requirements, were not considered "as people capable of acquiring rights and transmitting them."[100] According to this source, abortivos, then, possessed souls, but did not possess legal rights. And although the *Diccionario* declared abortion illicit and immoral in most circumstances, it also observed that "it is licit for the mother to take medication, drinks, etc. that she takes principally for her own health, when this is the only means of maintaining her health, even though an indirect affect on the animated fetus may be feared."[101] Even this Catholic publication, then, opined that, under certain circumstances, abortion was licit.

Political scientist Adriana Ortiz-Ortega argues that one reason why the church's position on abortion was muted in Mexico in the late nineteenth century was that the church and state had forged an unspoken "gentlemen's agreement" in the context of the church's diminished power in the face of liberal anticlericalism. This agreement, cemented at the time of the creation of the 1871 penal code, "led to the state's compensating for the liberalization of abortion laws with secrecy and a failure to implement the legal options and services that could be available to women."[102] Ortiz-Ortega sees the Catholic Church's contemporaneous weakness in Mexico as key to understanding why it did not oppose even those elements that allowed for a more lenient legal treatment of abortion in the 1871 code, even though the church in other locales, including in Spain, objected much more vocally to the liberalization of abortion laws.[103] However, she writes that since the Catholic Church retained considerable social power, the Mexican state "did not forcefully endorse abortion laws or other forms of law which would deter Catholic control."[104] Although Ortiz-Ortega does not detail which elements of abortion law the state failed to support, there is some evidence that this may refer to the rise of surgical abortions—abortos provocados or partos prematuros provocados—that medical professionals increasingly performed in the closing decades of the nineteenth century. The 1871 code permitted such practices when they existed to save the lives of pregnant women, but their enactment was and remains largely obscured.

Surgical Abortions

Despite this obscurity various sources from the last decades of the nineteenth century suggest that a portion of medical professionals consistently performed surgical abortions in the closing decades of the nineteenth century, although, due to their secretive nature, we cannot know the annual or total numbers of the operations undertaken. Physician Pedro Felipe Monlau's 1865 *Libro de los casados* (Book of married couples), a Spanish text that circulated in Mexico and roundly condemned intentional abortions, provided an exhaustive list of nonrecommended abortion practices, thereby suggesting that all were popularly attempted. They included "emetics, purgatives, sudorifics, diuretics, mercurial, more and less potent vomitives, emmenagogues, jumping, walking, blows, violent contusions, horseback riding, carriage riding, injections, perforations, forced dilations, Greek pessaries, strong moral sentiments, rue, juniper, chamomile, safran, ferrous preparations, cantharides, and *secule cornutum* [ergot]."[105] None, he believed, worked effectively. Even this text, however, conceded that, under specific circumstances, it was licit for physicians to perform a "parto prematuro" if the pregnant woman's pelvis would prevent delivery, or in cases of edema, heart aneurisms, or any other potentially fatal condition in the pregnant woman.[106]

Elizabeth O'Brien has recently examined the history of late nineteenth-century Mexican physicians who provided surgical or medicinal abortions in a manner that challenges Ortiz-Ortega's notion of the "gentlemen's agreement" between church and state limiting the availability of abortions. O'Brien comments that Mexican doctors allied themselves with the liberal reform project, including its secularist objectives. Among other works she studies physician Francisco Menocal's 1869 thesis *Estudio sobre el aborto en México* (Study of abortion in Mexico). Although his text was largely focused on the discussion of unintentional misbirths, O'Brien asserts that Menocal subtly opposed the papacy's 1869 condemnation of abortion as sinful in his assertion that the product of a woman's conception should only be referred to as an "egg" until the third month, when it became an "embryo" and then transformed into a "fetus" in the fourth month.[107] Indeed, this is the same language routinely used in both late nineteenth-century tracts and in the 1871 penal code, which referred to embryos and fetuses as "productos de concepcíon." In the decades that followed, some physicians used even more explicit language that suggests they did not consider embryos or fetuses as "people." In 1898 Juan Breña, in his defense of the duties and rights of physicians to perform therapeutic abortions discussed in this chapter's opening, included a lengthy discussion of the status of the unborn fetus, noting that the eighteenth-century French anatomist Marie François Xavier Bichat had viewed animal fetuses as "nula" (valueless), and observing that great numbers of subsequent doctors had argued that if its development were interrupted, "the fetus suffers no real prejudice since it loses a life of which it had not the slightest consciousness."[108]

The medical assessment that fetuses did not participate in humanity was also occasionally represented in abortion trials. In one 1902 abortion case originating in Valladolid, Yucatán, the court investigated Rudesindo May for the clandestine burial of an aborted embryo. Physicians interviewed in the trial declared that "during the first three months, the product of gestation does not present in any human form, nor is it viable, and it can be confused with coagulations or bloody concretions."[109] Since the civil registry referred to penalties for the clandestine burial only of human cadavers, the judge in this case declared May innocent, since he had not buried a cadaver that had a human form.

While Menocal's 1869 text focused primarily on the reasons why Mexican women were prone to miscarrying their fetuses accidentally, his tract was followed by others that discussed the medical procedures involved in intentionally provoking preterm deliveries, many of which O'Brien discusses in her fascinating treatment of physicians' facilitation of "Artificial Premature Births."[110] These included Eduardo Navarro y Cardona's (1873) thesis *Del parto prematuro en México y de las maneras con que se la provocado* (On preterm childbirth in Mexico and on the ways that it can be provoked). This work discussed the surgical procedure for the extraction of "legally viable" fetuses (understood as those over six months' gestation) in preterm pregnancies when birth at full term would be medically unadvisable, including for such conditions as vices of the formation of the pelvis, rickets, osteomalacia, chronic illness, and nervous accidents.[111] Navarro y Cardona narrated the details of several individual Mexican women's experiences with artificial preterm childbirth, including one twenty-eight-year-old from the capital who suffered from various debilitating conditions, including intestinal maladies and fevers, and who had endured several miscarriages and one horrific late-term misbirth.[112] To assist her in the successful delivery of a subsequent pregnancy, her attending doctors attempted to provoke the birth in advance of its "natural" timing by applying dilatory sponges to her cervix, breaking the membranes, and extracting the fetus by use of forceps. The newborn died eighteen hours later. One year later they attempted the operation again, provoking contractions by injecting water into her uterus, and eventually by a podalic inversion (the manual turning of the fetus inside the uterus before a breech delivery) and the use of forceps. In this instance both the mother and infant survived. In a second case of artificial preterm childbirth that Navarro y Cardona described, the birthing woman survived, but "the product arrived in a state of apparent death."[113] Shortly thereafter, however, the newborn revived. In a third case, both parties survived. In another, in which a woman suffering from eclampsia was pregnant with twins, the procedure of dilating the cervix and provoking labor through the administration of injections of water, followed by the extraction of the products with surgical instruments, saved the life of pregnant woman but of neither fetus.[114] In total Navarro y Cardona described ten operations of artificial preterm childbirth procedures. Of these the pregnant woman survived the procedure in eight cases, although, in one instance, a woman died twenty-five days after the operation. *Productos* perished in four out of ten instances.

Although many of the procedures Navarro y Cardona described were intended to save the lives of both the pregnant woman and the fetus she carried, Elizabeth O'Brien observes that, given that fetuses "surgically birthed" at six or seven months' gestation were unlikely to survive, the concept of artificial preterm birth "obscured the likelihood of survival, perhaps deliberately."[115] O'Brien also notes that physicians in other contexts, including the United States, Brazil, and Chile, referred to the procedure as "therapeutic abortions." And the growth of medical theses and discourses treating the subject of the performance therapeutic abortions—or provoked preterm childbirth—certainly suggests that the procedures were common enough to warrant the attention and expertise of new members of the medical profession.[116] This is also suggested by her discussion of the 620 "uterine injection" abortions that she uncovered medical students reported performing in public clinics in Mexico between 1890 and 1936.[117]

Several other medical theses from the 1880s and 1890s similarly treated the methods and justifications for surgical abortions, although they sometimes used euphemistic language, perhaps induced to do so by the outraged coverage a few doctors like physician Antonio Abrego, criminally investigated for performing an abortion on his lover, Maria Barrera, who died of hemorrhage in Mexico City in 1898, received in the press.[118] In 1885 Luis Troconis y Alcalá published his thesis, *En los embarazos tiernos, cuál es el mejor procedimiento operatorio para efectuar la desocupación de la matriz?* (In early pregnancy, what is the best surgical procedure to effect the disoccupation of the womb?). In this work he discussed various means by which physicians could dilate the cervix and extract an embryo, to "desocupar" the womb, which Troconis y Alcalá also called to "desembarazar" (depregnify) the woman, although his discussion involved cases in which physicians were treating patients in whom miscarriages were already in progress.[119] Jesús Tajonar y Cardosa argued in his 1884 thesis, *Breve estudio comparativo entre la embriotamía y la operación cesárea* (Brief comparative study between the embryotomy and the caesarean operation), that it was preferable in cases of very difficult births, or even the eventual likelihood of such difficulties in cases of women with small pelvises, for physicians to perform a preemptive embryotomy, in which the fetus would certainly die, rather than an emergency caesarean, in which there was a chance both mother and infant might be saved. Since the mother's life had so much more value than the infant's, and since it was rare for both parties to survive the caesarean operation, he saw embryotomies as preferable since they posed little danger to laboring women.[120]

Discussion of surgical abortions, while a frequent subject of obstetrical study in the late nineteenth century, actually dated to decades earlier. Joaquín Escriche y Martín's foundational legal dictionary, first published in Spain in 1837 but widely used in Mexico through the nineteenth-century, took up the question at midcentury. In the third edition of his text, published in 1847 Escriche referred to research on the procedure published in 1834 in the *Gaceta médica de Madrid*. This text discussed a controversial procedure used elsewhere in Europe to provoke early labor in the eighth month of pregnancy in cases when a woman's narrow pelvis suggested that labor and delivery would threaten both the fetus's life and that of the woman herself.[121] The *Gaceta* writers opined that no physician had the right to "risk the life of the fetus" and argued that it was imprudent to provoke labor and delivery before the fetus was viable.

Liberal political views dating back to midcentury, however, supported the notion that women possessed the right to terminate pregnancies that endangered their lives. As one liberal commentator in Mexico observed, quoting Jesuit writer N. Airault in an 1855 column published in *El monitor republicano*, "If the product [*fruto* in the original] is already animated and the mother will die with the infant, before she goes into labor, she should take remedies even though these might indirectly injure the product [of conception]." Women whose reputations would be harmed by an unwanted pregnancy, in the view of this writer, could also lawfully abort to protect their honor, "which is much more precious than life itself."[122]

By the late nineteenth century, many doctors, including David Cruz, believed that while provoked abortions (those occurring before seven months' gestation) were immoral, preterm provoked births were moral when conditions called for them.[123] Others, most notably physicians Juan María Rodríguez and Luis Hidalgo y Carpio (the latter who had presented a defense of the procedure to the Academia de Medicina in 1852), supported therapeutic abortions performed before seven months.[124] Hidalgo y Carpio and Gustavo Ruiz y Sandoval asserted that therapeutic abortions were lawful and necessary under particular circumstances. They discussed various methods of "physical manoeuvres" that might induce abortions, including the rupturing of the amniotic sac by any sharp object, dilation of the cervix to provoke contractions, or injections into the uterus by means of a syringe to detach the fertilized egg from the uterus.[125] They observed that the "Método de Tarnier"—the separation of the membranes and the induction of uterine contractions—would be used illegally because it required particular medical instruments and a certain level of skill.[126] They also discussed how medicinal treatments might induce abortions, commenting that the administration of juniper at a high dose was certain to provoke an abortion, while rue, according to a French physician writing in 1838, frequently displayed powerful abortive effects.[127]

One physician, J. Duque de Estrada, professor of obstetrics at the Escuela Nacional de Medicina, described his performance of a provoked aborto on a patient in an 1898 report published in the *Crónica médica Mexicana*.[128] His patient, a woman in the fourth month of pregnancy, suffered from *auto-intoxicación gravídica*, a condition so severe Estrada thought if he did not abort the fetus, the pregnancy was certain to kill her.[129] Having disinfected her vagina and cervix, he used forceps and the introduction of successively large probes to dilate her cervix, at which point "my finger could fully penetrate the cervix and the cavity behind it; having done this and bringing my finger between the egg and the uterine wall, I started to dislodge the egg at its lateral edges." Estrada was able, eventually, to extract the "product" whole, along with the placenta and membranes. He assessed his patient as having responded perfectly to the operation, which provoked no hemorrhaging or local infection. Nevertheless he reported that by the third day after the operation, although she presented no fever, blood, or apparent infection, he found his patient in great pain. She perished the following day, which he attributed not to the abortion but to the "terrible *intoxicación*" that had first threatened her pregnancy.[130] Elsewhere Estrada advocated for physicians' need to lawfully perform embryotomies, which the Mexican School of Medicine had outlawed years earlier, in cases when a fetus was certain of dying and a woman would be more traumatized by the performance of a podalic inversion than by the removal of the embryo in pieces with forceps or other instruments.[131]

Discussions of misbirths and induced abortions appeared frequently in the last decades of the nineteenth century within the emergent field of forensic "legal" medicine. Medical expertise on questions surrounding virginity, reproduction, and birth had long played a role in court cases involving rape, illegitimacy, abortion, and infanticide. Such matters became ever more central to the field of legal medicine in the closing decades of the century. In 1871 one of two deciding questions that two candidates had to address in their competition to secure the chair of legal medicine in the capital's Mexican School of Medicine treated the issue of "criminal abortion."[132] The state formally recognized the expertise of legal medicine experts with the 1880 creation of the Legal Medical Counsel, whose purpose was to inform "judges and magistrates on all medico-legal questions that might be aired before the courts and that had an ambiguous or difficult nature in the judgment of the respective authority."[133] The question had become urgent in part, as Laura Shelton observes, because physicians in this era continued to have great difficulty distinguishing between induced abortions or accidental miscarriages.[134]

The ubiquity of medicinal or surgical abortions at this time is also suggested by the fact of commonplace newspaper advertisements for medical remedies to address the effects of either abortion or miscarriage. The "Consultorio Benevolent," for example, advertised its services in the capital city in a 1908 edition of *El Heraldo Médico* with a list of therapeutic specialties and medicines available, beginning with several elixirs to treat "symptoms of abortion."[135] A short advertisement in a 1916 classified section of *El Pueblo* advertised the services of midwives who could assist in "births, abortions, intrauterine or hypodermic injections," and who provided "secret cures, etc."[136]

Conclusion

Outside of the field of reproductive history, scholars, journalists, artists, and others consider the period between 1870 and 1930 one of dramatic change in Mexico. The country moved from the positivist, dictatorial, European-oriented Porfirian era through a dramatic ten-year revolution, to the establishment of a socialist-oriented, incorporationist, and ostensibly secular state. Conventional periodization within the field of Mexican history normally adopts a central division between the Porfirian and postrevolutionary eras.

This chapter's examination of a sixty-year period beginning in 1871 reveals that, in terms of the history of abortion, although this era did present some dramatic developments from the long period that preceded it, much less change occurred within the era from 1871 to 1930. The legal regulations on abortion established by the Distrito Federal's 1871 penal code broke in significant ways from viceregal and early republican legal treatments of abortion. But once established, few changes separated the revolutionary era from the Porfirian one in terms of conceptions of abortion. Indeed, neither did the first post-revolutionary legal codes discussed at the beginning of this chapter institute dramatic change in its regulation. Anti-abortion Catholic perspectives of the act are most conspicuous by their absence from public discourse across this entire period. Denunciations of the practice of abortion rose in Mexico in the 1880s and remained significantly higher than earlier in the century, but convictions for the crime remained infrequent across time. We see other continuities from earlier eras in terms of the demographic portrait of those accused of procuring abortions, and in the methods women used to abort pregnancies, which often involved inducing preterm miscarriages through the ingestion of plant-based medicines.

Another significant transformation apparent in the period between 1870 and 1930 from earlier eras, although one that does not appear to have changed greatly within the space of the Porfirian-revolutionary eras, was the introduction and institutionalization of the practice of surgical abortions. While, elsewhere in North America, the closing decades of the nineteenth century witnessed the growth of a physician-led movement to restrict women's access to both medicinal and surgical abortion, the opposite occurred in Mexico. As O'Brien observes, in Mexico physicians tacitly accepted and participated in "fertility control that was couched in a social salvational rhetoric that alternatively heeded, reformed, or rejected Catholic reproductive doctrines."[137] Medical theses, newspaper coverage, and scholarly publications all demonstrate that many doctors, committed to saving women whose lives or health were endangered by their pregnancies or prospective acts of giving birth, dedicated their energy and research expertise to refining techniques and teaching younger generations of students about the most efficient methods for provoking and executing term and preterm surgical abortions.

3

1931–2000

At the 1952 annual meeting of the Assembly of Mexican Surgeons, two physicians, Luis Carrillo Azcárate and Joaquín Correa Cedillo, from the Mexican Academy of Medicine, announced a startling new perspective on the morality of abortion. Rejecting the position held by both late nineteenth-century legal medicine and moral theology, that a physician's obligation was to preserve a pregnant woman's life above that of her offspring, Carrillo and Correa proclaimed that the organization they represented had resolved that "in no moment can it be accepted that the life of the mother takes priority over that of the child."[1] Their announcement marked a moment of change within circles of institutional medicine in Mexico, which retreated in the early 1950s from decades of tacit support for the performance of surgical abortions to adopt a much more critical attitude toward the practice. Many practitioners and professional organizations continued to follow suit in subsequent decades. Ironically, however, this movement toward greater condemnation of abortion within the field of medicine occurred simultaneously with criminal courts' less frequent prosecution of the act. Although abortion laws did not change dramatically in Mexico between 1931 and the late 1970s, the rates at which community members denounced women, and at which the state prosecuted them, declined at about the same time as abortion became more medically contentious.

This chapter surveys the changes to abortion's legality and accessibility in the period from 1929 until 2000 by considering legal codes, medical issues, religious views, feminist activism, and popular attitudes. All of these factors influenced the changing dimensions of abortion across the twentieth century, sometimes in unexpected ways. This chapter draws from a wealth of published scholarship on this history.[2] Although earlier chapters were organized thematically, this final chapter treats this history chronologically because this is the easiest way to show how the complex facets of this history shaped one another in its unrolling across this period.

With one important exception, many aspects of abortion law in Mexico went largely unchanged from 1871 until the late 1970s, when local legislators initiated sporadic and geographically uneven liberalization of state penal codes that continued into the early twenty-first century. The Federal District took more dramatic steps toward the decriminalization of first-trimester abortion in 2000 and 2007. Many other Mexican states responded with legislative rejections of these, accompanied by a rise in prosecution for the crime following the pronounced dwindling of abortion's prosecution in the period from the 1940s through the 1990s.

In the realm of medicine, the country's twentieth-century experience followed a different pattern, whereby physicians performed and publicized medicinal and surgical abortions more freely in the first half of the twentieth century and then, institutionally, adopted an increasingly critical position about the performance of "therapeutic abortions," beginning in the early 1950s. During the 1970s and 1980s, as abortion began to become an issue of greater public focus, some individual physicians continued supporting the practice, but the medical profession as a whole retreated from advocacy or even much public discussion of abortion. What may appear as the other most dramatic medical innovation in terms of late twentieth-century abortion—the growth of pharmaceutical abortions, which did not necessitate surgical intervention—might instead be understood as a continuity of women's preconquest, colonial, and nineteenth-century practice of exerting reproductive control through the ingestion of plant-based abortifacients.

Two groups—feminist activists and Catholic organizations—influenced abortion's legal, medical, and political dimensions in the twentieth century in ways that had not occurred earlier. Although both groups began organizing and lobbying to either further liberalize or impede women's access abortion in the 1930s, neither one of them effected abortion legislation nor altered its accessibility in this period. Advocacy on both sides of the abortion debate was fairly dormant in Mexico until feminist groups began organizing around the issue again in the late 1970s. Their actions, in turn, spurred a growth of militancy among Catholic lay and episcopal groups. The latter became particularly vocal at important moments in legal debates over abortion in different states, particularly in Chiapas (1990), Guanajuato (1999), and Mexico City (2000).[3]

Constancy and Change, 1930s–40s

One remarkable element of the treatment of abortion in the Federal District's first penal code was its endurability; its articles remained largely unaltered for 130 years after 1871. In 1903 Porfirian penologist Miguel S. Macedo established a commission to revise the code, but the 1912 revision that his commission produced contained only minor modifications, and none affected abortion.[4] The Federal District's postrevolutionary 1929 penal code, commissioned by President Plutarco Elías Calles, did contain some departures form the 1871 provisions. One innovation in was its handling of crimes committed by medical professionals specifying that doctors, surgeons, and midwives required the express permission of patients, or those responsible for them, in order to perform any potentially dangerous procedure, or risk arrest, imprisonment, fines, and the suspension of their licenses.[5]

Specifically with respect to abortion, the 1929 code contained some other, though minor, novelties. While the new code, like its predecessor, defined abortion as the "extraction of the product of conception or its provoked expulsion by any means," the 1871 code had specified that such an act was only considered an abortion when the expulsion "was done without necessity," implying that there were occasions when which abortion was necessary and therefore lawful. This language was omitted from the 1929 code, which also introduced for the first time the notion that such an interruption served to interrupt the "life" of the product of conception.[6] Like its antecedent, however, the new code labeled the procedure a *parto prematuro artificial*, if performed after the beginning of the eighth month of gestation, and declared that such operations would not be penalized if, in the absence of their performance, "the pregnant woman runs the risk of death in the judgment of her attending doctor, who should seek the opinion of a second doctor."[7] The code continued to declare nonpunishable all abortions provoked "accidentally by the pregnant woman," and it eliminated the discussion of the attenuating circumstances involving the maintenance of sexual honor that had featured in the 1871 code, although it maintained these in its discussion of infanticide, and the 1931 code produced almost immediately afterward reintroduced the honor clauses verbatim. The 1929 code also differed from the 1871 code in that it slightly reduced the prison sentences for those convicted of making a woman abort "without physical or moral violence" to three (down from four) years "segregation" irrespective of attenuating or extenuating circumstances.

The 1931 code, produced at the behest of the legal establishment—which, Robert Buffington observes, criticized the 1929 code as "inconsistent, unnecessarily radical, and unacceptably practical"—contained a significant change respecting abortion.[8] For the first time, abortions were not punishable when the pregnancy was the result of rape. Mexico apparently included this clause to modernize its code in accordance with norms many European nations had adopted after World War I to address the large numbers of women raped and impregnated by invading soldiers.[9] The 1931 code referred for the first time to the "death" of the product of conception "in any moment of pregnancy."[10] It also reduced the punishments for women who aborted for "honorable causes" from two years to between six months and one year.

Finally, the 1931 code, produced within the era in which many state and scientific communities in Mexico were experimenting with the pseudoscience of eugenics, introduced another novel element to its treatment of abortion, specifying that, if performed because either the product of conception or the pregnant woman ran the risk of death if not undertaken, it was licit for physicians to perform a parto premature artificial.[11] This article, which, Olga Islas de González Mariscal points out, became subsequently known as "eugenic abortion" (because it might refer to grave medical conditions in the fetus), provided the legal foundation for subsequent state codes, many of them introduced in the 1970s, that allowed for abortions in cases where the product of conception was medically nonviable.[12]

Most Mexican states adopted the 1931 Federal District code without dramatic modification in its wake, and most state penal codes, like that of the Federal District code, remained fairly stable until the late 1970s. Three exceptions appeared in the states of Yucatán, Chihuahua, and Chiapas, all of which modified the 1931 code in their 1938 adoptions of it to include clauses decriminalizing (or lightening the sentence, in the case of Chiapas) instances when women in dire economic circumstances aborted their pregnancies. In the case of Yucatán, abortion was legalized when women in economic difficulty were already mother to three children or more.[13]

Yucatán's reception to such situations may have arisen from its history of socialist organizing. In the early twentieth century, socialist and feminist leaders assumed prominence on the peninsula. In 1916 Mérida, Yucatán, hosted the country's first feminist congress, an event organized by the state's socialist governor Salvador Alvarado, along with politicians Elvia Carrillo Puerto and her brother, the state's future governor, Felipe Carrillo Puerto.[14] The 1916 congress focused on expanding female education and female suffrage, principally at the municipal level. Journalist and activist Hermila Galindo did not attend the 1916 congress but composed a speech that was read aloud during the proceedings. Attendees were scandalized by Galindo's discussion of the sexual double standard that condemned women but not men who engaged in extramarital sex: "How often does the newspaper print an account of this or that unhappy young woman who, to hide her error, resorted to the crime of killing her own child?" she asked. "Criminal statistics are full of cases of infanticide and provoked abortion, and do note even count the many hidden cases, demonstrating how powerful the grief of public vindication can be in the soul of the sad delinquent woman!"[15] Alaíde Fopp writes that Galindo's introduction of this topic attempted to take the congress in a direction many of the middle class school teachers who attended were not prepared to go, and that her text was "immediately labeled immoral and denied inclusion in the records of the congress."[16] Some contemporaries, nevertheless, evidently agreed with Galindo. The following year, however, the Regional Workers Convention held in Tampico in 1917 recognized workers' right to prevent "unlimited procreation."[17]

Feminist organizers in Yucatán continued their work into the next decade, promoting their ties to international figures. The American birth control activist Margaret Sanger traveled to Mexico five times in the early postrevolutionary period to help publicize information about contraception. In 1922, with the support of Governor Carrillo Puerto, Sanger published five thousand copies of a pamphlet called *The Compass of the Home*, informing women about home remedies that women might use to control natality (although disavowing abortion); ten thousand more copies were issued in a second edition.[18]

By the early 1930s, socialist, communist, and feminist organizations made more national inroads, including with the 1935 foundation of the Frente Único

Pro Derechos de la Mujer (United Front for Women's Rights), a coalition that eventually boasted a membership of fifty thousand and was supported by the Mexican Communist Party. And in 1936 several abortion depenalization advocates, including physicians Matilde Rodríguez Cabo, Esther Chapa, and Ofelia Domínguez Navarro, along with communist organizers Refugio García and Esperanza Balmaceda, attended the National Convention for the Unification of Penal Legislation that President Lázaro Cardenás convened in an effort to render uniform the nation's diverse state penal codes.[19] Drawing inspiration from Communist Russia, which had decriminalized abortion in 1920 (although it would recriminalize it in 1936), these figures pointed to the economic factors that prompted women's need for legal abortion. The following year, Rodríguez Cabo, Mexico's first female psychiatrist, who also played an active role in the state's Ministry of Health and Welfare programs of the mid-1930s, also unsuccessfully proposed abortion's decriminalization and the foundation of state regulation of abortion to the Socialist Front of Lawyers, but there, too, depenalization advocates failed to make legislative or judicial inroads.[20]

Supporters of abortion in the 1930s and 1940s, as well as drawing inspiration from the Soviet model, also came from the field of eugenics. Adherents of Mexico's eugenic movement encouraged state intervention in the arenas of reproduction, health, and childcare for the purposes of strengthening the population, in order to eliminate the retrograde influences of the physically, psychologically, or socially deviant: alcoholics, drug addicts, those infected by venereal disease, those with criminal tendencies, and those deemed less racially desirable.[21] As Beatriz Urías Horcasitas observes, concern in this period with combating social degeneration prompted the establishment of various state programs supporting aid for maternal and newborn health as well as those calling for mandated prenuptial medical exams and proposals to sterilize criminals and the mentally ill.[22] Indeed, the founders of the Mexican Eugenics Society itself emerged from within a section of the Mexican Society of Puericulture, established in 1929.[23] In the late 1930s and 1940s, such considerations also contributed to the entrenchment of female sexuality within the marital sphere, where its expression was reserved exclusively for reproductive purposes. In the 1940s and 1950s, lay Catholic organizations, including Acción Católica (Catholic Action), advocated for the eradication of sexual libertinage they believed accompanied Mexican modernity, and women's greater financial and economic independence.[24]

Although in 1933 the Mexican Eugenics Society condemned abortion as reprehensible, leftists and eugenicists sometimes converged in their support for abortion.[25] The founding member of the Mexican Eugenics Society, surgeon and professor of medicine at the UNAM Alfredo Saavedra, discussed this confluence in a criminological article dating from 1938. Saavedra described how physician Rafael Carrillo, professor of the School of Medicine and founder of the of the Mexican Puericulture Society, and Marxist Matilde Rodríguez Cabo both opined that social and psychological circumstances constituted a justification for abortion. These included "economic conditions, numerous offspring, pre-existent illnesses in the pregnant women, age, and a frank anti-maternal sentiment."[26] Saavedra asserted that Carrillo and Rodríguez Cabo extended the justification for lawful abortion to more explicitly eugenic considerations, including "physical or mental defects transmissible by inheritance."[27] However, some eugenicists strove to distance themselves from associations with political leftists. In 1930 Catholic doctor Manuel Escontria had published a lengthy critical discussion in the *Gaceta médica de México* (Mexican medical gazette) titled "Eugenics and Limits on Natality." He opposed the idea of the eugenic justifications for limiting childbirth as a form of propaganda that the Mexican state produced in its distorted admiration for the Russian model. Escontria derided eugenic support for abortion not because of its racist agenda, but because of its connotations of libertinage and moral laxity.[28]

Physician Bernardo J. Gastélum, former head of the national Department of Health and Public Assistance, began a 1934 article published in Yucatán's *Revista médica* (Medical review) on surgical abortion with a circuitous discussion of the economic justification for doctors' performance of such operations. He observed that the inhabitants of a healthy society required sufficient income for their subsistence, as well as "diversion, sport, culture, and social relations," to achieve social harmony. Without them countries would be wracked with class struggle.[29] In the same way, Gastélum continued, the healthy functioning of families was also based on their economic outlook, where "one child more often complicates a family's budget," disturbing its tranquility.[30] If a family grew indefinitely, this could lead to the death of "a great majority of children."

To avoid such situations, he observed, many families resorted to abortion to control the birth rates in their homes.[31]

Intriguingly for a respected state functionary, Gastélum sidestepped the discussion of the legal implications of performing abortions in such circumstances and moved directly into a detailed description of the surgical procedure itself, an area of medicine he said that should be known to not only specialists in urban centers but also to general practitioners, particularly in small communities. He observed that women in the second month of pregnancy often visited midwives or doctors who "ordinarily practice the brutal procedure of puncturing the egg."[32] Brutal as they might be, Gastélum commented that such "ovular abortions" were frequently realized "without incident." As the embryo further developed, however, abortions that did not provoke unwanted complications required more skill. Such operations, as he detailed, involved dilating the cervix with "Hegar's candles" (*las bujías de Hegar*), sterilizing the vulva, introducing one or two fingers through the cervix, and then using them to separate the placenta from the uterine wall, after which the placenta could be extracted whole from the uterus, an action that terminated the pregnancy.

Eugenics influenced Gastélum to support the performance of surgical abortions, but other politicians and civil servants in this era generally operationalized eugenics in more abstract measures, including in puericulture programs and campaigns to control venereal disease and prostitution. Further, Alexandra Stern discovered that eugenics prompted the state of Veracruz to pass a 1937 law legalizing and encouraging the sterilization of biologically undesirable procreators.[33] In addition to Veracruz, my examination of early twentieth-century state penal codes revealed that the state of Sonora, exceptionally, passed a "eugenic" clause much earlier than many other states. In its 1940 adaptation of the Federal District's 1931 code, Sonora declared that those convicted of abortion should be sentenced from between two and eight years' imprisonment, but that such operations were licit in cases of rape, when a woman's life was threatened in its absence, or "when the expulsion of the fetus is due to eugenic considerations."[34] Although such considerations did not appear in Yucatán's penal code, that state's 1938 Constitution did use similar language, commenting that in the interest of promoting the healthy reproduction of its population and the elimination of the "degeneration of the species," the state would establish medical clinics devote to voluntary sterilization of individuals at risk of engendering "weak or abnormal beings."[35] Chiapas's 1938 Constitution contained similar language.

While socialists and eugenicists supported expanding access to abortion in the 1930s, a counterreaction to such ideas also developed in this decade from within the Catholic Church. Elizabeth Maier points out that the Catholic Church's twentieth-century opposition to abortion is rooted in three tenets that abortion violates: "Human life as divine intervention, procreation as the basic function and sacred obligation of marriage, and motherhood as women's primary mission."[36] In the early part of the century, local actors in Mexico occasionally expressed objections to abortion on one or more of these such grounds. A Catholic lay group active in Yucatán in the early twentieth century, the Caballeros de Colón, for instance, pressured state authorities to prosecute the press for publishing Margaret Sanger's 1922 birth control booklet.[37] However, stronger directives in this period that explicitly focused on abortion came from abroad. The papacy took up the issue in 1930 with the publication of *Casti Connubii* (Of chaste wedlock), an encyclical Pope Pius XI issued that stressed the sanctity of marriage, prohibited Catholics from using birth control, and reiterated the church's prohibition on abortion. Pius XI developed his decree in response to social transformations in Europe in an era of rising divorce rates, movements toward abortion's decriminalization, and growing tolerance for homosexuality.

Mexican bishops, although committed to enforcing *Casti Connubii*, were curtailed from doing so effectively by the secularist revolutionary and post-revolutionary governments. Article 130 of the 1917 Constitution formalized the church's exclusion from the political realm, while Article 3 required the country's education system to be secular. Such measures prevented church officers from formally addressing legislative changes that conservatives believed threatened the family. The federal state's 1917 family law reforms allowed women greater financial and legal independence and facilitated divorce while the 1928 civil code specified the equality of the sexes before the law and denied women's subordination to their husbands in marriage.[38] Despite his constitutional obligation to refrain from political involvement, in 1931 the Mexican archbishop Pascual Díaz wrote a strong defense of *Casti Connubii* and worked to develop a network of anti-communist political groups whose supporters fought both in the Cristero uprising of 1928 and were instrumental in the 1939 foundation of the Partido de Acción Nacional (Party of National Action, or PAN).[39] Although the archbishop's directive and the party's message of rigid marital fixity found willing reception in such groups as the Unión Nacional de Padres de Familia (National Union of Heads of Household), which had formed in 1917, the focus on abortion was marginal to their discussions. The archival catalog of the Union de Padres de Familia mentions only one document relating to abortion, and this was a "ProVida file" dating from 1989.[40] So, while the broad social idea of championing maternity as destiny had profound implications for Mexican politics and society in the twentieth century, the explicit focus of Catholic organizing over the issue of abortion in the 1930s was limited. Elizabeth O'Brien reports that, while the archbishop's message of support for *Casti Connubii* was read at masses throughout Mexico, the encyclical left a light documentary record; it generated no discussion in contemporary news dailies, and no successful legislative campaigns developed in Mexico in its wake.[41]

From the 1920s through the 1940s, despite Catholic objections to abortion, many Mexican doctors published articles defending the medical justification for abortion, most often in order to preserve the life or health of pregnant women. Physician Fernando Narváez, writing in the *Revista médica de Yucatán* (Medical review of Yucatán) in 1943, observed, for example, that in a limited number of cases, "the interruption of gestation was justified," specifying that such was the case when a therapeutic abortion was the only way to save the life of a woman when the continuation of pregnancy threatened to kill her or to harm her vital organs.[42] While noting that abortion in the first trimester was normally uncomplicated, Narváez focused on the more dangerous second-trimester procedures, which included provoking an abortion "by means of mechanical agents (probes, *laminarias*, or gauze wicks) and once labor is established, rupturing the membranes and administering oxytocins."[43] Because such procedures often produced infections or required repetition in order to ensure the extraction of all elements of conception, Narváez endorsed a method E. A. Boero had publicized in 1935, involving the use of a syringe to extract amniotic fluid from the uterus, replacing the fluid with an injection of formaldehyde. Narváez praised the efficiency of the procedure, which caused little physical trauma and presented a low chance of infection. He also remarked that it was admirable because it could be done "without the patient realizing it, which is greatly important because it avoids emotional trauma," implying that this form of eugenically inspired procedure was frequently done on patients without their knowledge or consent.[44] He concluded by reporting that a colleague, Pedro Villalobos, had recently successfully performed the procedure on a woman suffering from cardiac ailments. In his 1936 thesis, another Mexico City physician, Ciro Ruíz Culebro, took an even stronger position, as Elizabeth O'Brien discusses, advocating for abortion's depenalization for the first four months after gestation.[45]

A third physician, Fernando Perera Castillo, professor of clinical surgery at the Universidad Nacional de México, published an article on the place of surgery in abortions in 1951, when the institutional consensus was already moving to condemn physicians' provisions of abortions as illicit and illegal, despite their ongoing legality under certain conditions in penal codes. Perera Castillo discussed procedures for surgical intervention in instances of both unintentional miscarriages and intentional abortions, asserting that such care should be extended to women suffering from complications of abortions initiated outside of hospital settings when a portion of the product of conception remained in the uterus: "In our service in Ward 8 of this Hospital [Juárez], more than 80 percent of the patients are admitted with *riletrorragias* occasioned by abortions that they have tried to hide, omitting to tell us important information crucial to their diagnoses."[46] In such cases Perera Castillo provided advice for the use of obstetrical surgery, most often the "uterine curettage" to complete the extraction or address the hemorrhaging.[47] Other articles published in the late 1940s defended the medical practice of providing therapeutic abortion as lawful and declared that the procedure should be legalized for economic as well as medical reasons.[48] Physicians and midwives who provided abortions in these and other circumstances provoked the state and social critique in the 1940s and 1950s, although it is difficult to say how widespread their activities were.[49]

The Static Midcentury, 1950s–60s

Mexican abortion law remained unaltered through the midcentury decades, a period during which there was little evidence of strong public advocacy either for or against abortion. Three drafted plans (*anteproyectos*) for the Distrito Federal's penal code dating from 1949, 1958, and 1963, which Adriana Ortiz-Ortega comments were initiated by Catholic "conservative forces," would have each increased the punishments for those convicted of the crime, but these

Table 3. Abortos listed in the TSJDF catalog, 1930–79

DECADE	NUMBER OF CASES	DETAILS
1930–39	106	Includes 5 *tentative*, 1 *provocado*
1940–49	90	Includes 4 *tentative*
1950–59	9	Includes 1 *clandestino*
1960–69	21	

Source: Created by the author from the TSJDF catalog.

were never implemented.[50] Furthermore, existent sources suggest that criminal prosecution of abortion diminished from the 1940s through to 2000. Historians searching for twentieth-century criminal cases have located only a handful of these at midcentury. Saydi Núñez located six abortion cases in the TSJDF series between 1920 and 1940, and Martha Santillán Esqueda uncovered nineteen women prosecuted for abortion in Mexico City between 1940 and 1950.[51] As indicated in table 3, the catalog records of the Tribunal Superior de Justicia del Distrito Federal, housed in the Archivo General de la Nación, likewise lists diminishing numbers of judicial cases involving investigations for the crime of aborto across the twentieth century. The actual number of cases involving intentional abortions is likely even smaller than those recorded in the TSJDF catalog, since these records no doubt include cases of accidental abortions induced though domestic violence.

Other sources support the characterization of the diminishment of prosecution for abortion after the 1930s. The Public Ministry of Mexico City recorded, for instance, that in 1935 courts prosecuted 13 cases of abortion (compared to 381 cases of homicide).[52] A *Gaceta médica de México* article from 1932 claimed that approximately ten thousand Mexican women aborted criminally every year, while only three were prosecuted every decade.[53] Midcentury newspapers infrequently reported the crime and included stories of doctors imprisoned for it as frequently as pregnant women themselves. In one of these, the Guadalajara's daily paper *El Informador* reported that in Mazatlán, Sinaloa, the state had investigated two doctors in July 1939 in the case of a woman who had died of puerperal fever caused by an "aborto provocado."[54] One 1954 news article from the same paper related that a criminal judge had ordered doctor Carlos Benavides Pérez along with a nurse and two other people imprisoned for the crimes of "homicide, abortion, and robbery, occasioned by the death of Gloria Basail Cardosa, who was operated upon to impede the arrival of her child." The paper also reported that "three lawyers called by the accused doctor declined to defend him having read the file."[55]

Prosecution for abortion remained low even in later periods, even as the rates of abortion were consistently high. The nationally circulating magazine *Sucesos Para Todos* (Events for everyone) ran a series of stories in 1971 on the current state of abortion in the country. It compiled statistics from ten medical institutions between 1963 and 1967, reporting a total of 11,499 abortions performed in this period. The magazine also noted that of 2,626 abortions it had studied in detail, 96 percent were "criminal" in that there was no medical or legal reason justifying them.[56] Lawyer Luis de la Barreda Solorzano, then president of the Federal District's Commission on Human Rights, asserted that in the late 1970s a state research group estimated conservatively that 800,000 abortions occurred annually nationwide.[57] One 1975 Mexico City study of 316 physicians who worked for the Centro Médico Nacional del Instituto Mexicano del Seguro Social revealed that over 83 percent of them had direct knowledge of at least one patient who had had an illegally induced abortion.[58] At the end of the following decade, the National Survey on Fertility and Health reported that one in six women of fertile age at that time in Mexico had had either miscarried or aborted.[59]

Nevertheless, in an interview published in 1994, Barreda Solorzano described abortion as "a crime that is not actually prosected," noting that while hundreds of thousands of women aborted every year, in 1988 only two defendants in the Mexican capital were jailed for abortion, while in 1989 six were jailed.[60] Barreda Solorzano observed that judges fined rather than jailed most of those convicted, in part to avoid further overcrowding of Mexican prisons. He also commented that the small numbers of those incarcerated was due to the fact that many women paid bribes to medical personnel or police to avoid having their crimes exposed. A 1996 study showed somewhat higher rates of denunciation for the crime: ninety-four denunciations in 1995 and fifty-four in 1996; however, courts pursued only a small fraction of these cases.[61]

The one aspect of abortion history that did undergo dramatic change at midcentury was the attitude institutional medicine adopted to the procedure and expressed in the resolutions of professional medical societies. By the early

1950s, doctors articulated increasing discomfort with the performance of "therapeutic" abortions. Physicians Enrique Viesca Benavides, Salvador Lara and Jesús Vales Muriel, who presented their views at the first National Reunion of Gynecology and Obstetrics in Monterrey in June 1950, condemned the practice of therapeutic abortion, asserting that "the repulsiveness and criminality of abortion is undeniable no matter the circumstances used to justify it or the excuses provided for it." They decried the fact of a country purposefully limiting its natality, which led it to "moral, economic, cultural, and social decadence."[62]

The three physicians characterized all abortions as "acts of homicide in which all the aggravating factors of premeditation, treachery, and self-interest are united" and postulated that although supporters claimed women often procured abortions out of economic desperation, the truth was that more often they did it out of "selfishness, guilty, vanity, cowardice, laziness, or malice."[63] Most of the rest of their presentation entailed the discussion (and dismissal) of the medical conditions, including tuberculosis, cancer, and repeated hemorrhaging, that doctors accepted as justifications for performing abortions. They suggested amending the penal code to require that cases of therapeutic abortions should only be unpenalized when the pregnant woman "ran the risk of death in the judgement of her attending doctor, who had to ALWAYS consult the opinion of two other specialists: surgeons, internists, and/or gynecologists."[64] Such an opinion should then be confirmed, they proposed, by the Medical College. They concluded with a set of suggestions that indicated they knew economic factors were related to the impossibility of child-rearing some Mexicans faced, but suggested that the government could address the situation by creating and subsidizing a system of state daycare, as well as subsidies for single mothers with more than three children, and a tax that would be imposed on single men over age twenty-five, as well as the elimination of the obligation to pay taxes for any head of household with over eight children.

At the same association's second meeting the following year, opposition to surgical abortions was even more pronounced. There doctor José G. Martinez from Monterrey's Society of Obstetrics and Gynecology suggested that physicians and medical organizations should no longer use the term "therapeutic abortions"—those undertaken for reasons that were "apparently legitimate"—because "the term abortion signified homicide in most cases."[65] Martinez, whose point of departure was that fetuses possessed a human soul from the moment of conception, declared that current medical advances meant that the need for therapeutic abortion was on the point of disappearing, so that it would no longer be necessary for doctors to "kill an innocent, with curative means."[66] He reported statistics from four American hospitals in the previous six years documenting eight thousand cases of women examined for prenatal care whose medical conditions qualified them for "interruption of pregnancy." However, he asserted that medical care other than therapeutic abortions had successfully addressed many of their medical conditions, including in cases of two women who had undergone caesarean births at six months' pregnancy. In both, the women and their babies survived. Other procedures, he noted (without specifying how many), had not ended successfully.[67] He concluded by declaring that "for the most part, or in the totality of Latin countries therapeutic abortion has ceased to be practiced."[68] Institutional criticism of abortion by 1952 had moved beyond the field of obstetrics and was also advocated, as discussed in this chapter's opening, by the Mexican Academy of Medicine.

El Porvenir, Monterrey's daily newspaper, reported in 1958 that the National Assembly of Surgeons had issued a declaration against Article 333 of the Federal District's penal code, which said that abortion caused by a pregnant woman's carelessness was not punishable.[69] That same year the prominent former public health director physician Bernardo Gastélum, who in 1934 had endorsed the necessity of medicinal abortions, including for economic and sociological reasons, adopted a dramatically different position fourteen years later in a paper he presented to the National Academy of Medicine in October 1958. Gastélum discussed how the international position in Europe and the Americas was that therapeutic abortion did not exist, noting that physician David Fregoso of the Hospital Juárez had recently commented: "For at least the past ten years, abortion has not been practiced for curative ends and there is no maternal, fetal, nor ovular condition that justifies it."[70] A second doctor, director of the state-run public Maternity Hospital No. 1, concurred: "Abortion is not practiced in any instance, and it is considered that indications for its performance at the present moment have practically disappeared."[71] The remainder of Gastélum's lengthy address involved a thoroughly referenced discussion of why, in light of recent scientific advances, no medical circumstances existed—not cancer, not hypertension, not heart disease—that made therapeutic abortions to save the life of the pregnant women necessary or even desirable under any circumstances. A speaker who followed Gastélum, physician Alcibiádes Marván, applauded Gastélum's conclusion.[72] In the discussion that followed, several others concurred, while only one voice, that of Manuel Mateos Fournier, who observed "at the present moment, abortion as therapy has diminished in great part, although not in totality," registered a slightly different view.[73]

Such a position may have become the institutional norm by 1952, but a minority of physicians continued to advocate for the legality of therapeutic abortions. This group included doctors Augusto Pérez Molina, Manuel Díaz Estua, and Abraham Bazán, all from the city of Veracruz, who advocated for the morality and legality of the operation, a position they acknowledged was "diametrically opposed to those of the majority," at the second national meeting of the Obstetrics and Gynecological Society of Veracruz in 1952.[74] The bulk of their justification involved the ongoing evidence of various medical conditions potentially fatal in pregnant women or that were destined to produce nonviable fetuses. These advocates of therapeutic abortion also indicated that there might be "social and economic considerations" that justified abortion, pointing out that Mexico suffered from a lack of education, resources, and sufficient medical care, and that "an immense majority of our population obtains with difficulty the economic resources necessary to satisfy their most urgent needs."[75] All of these factors, in their opinion, suggested that therapeutic abortions, while not ideal, remained necessary.

It is difficult to know precisely why prominent physicians and medical associations, which in earlier decades had supported the performance of therapeutic abortions, changed course in the 1950s. However, two broad changes in the state's relationship to the medical profession and to the Catholic Church offer partial explanations. First, according to Gustavo Nigenda and Armando Solórzano, the medical profession, which in earlier decades had successfully retained greater autonomy from the state, became more tightly incorporated into institutional structure, political will, and ideological orientation of the federal government, beginning with the presidency of Manuel Ávila Camacho (1940–46).[76] Second, although the Catholic Church would remain constitutionally barred from commenting on political matters until President Carlos Salinas's 1992 revocation of Article 130 of the 1917 Constitution, in Soledad Loaeza's analysis, Ávila Camacho's presidency also witnessed the beginning of a shift toward an ideological reconciliation between church and state such that both institutions recognized points of mutual self-interest, including the fact that "the model of socialization of Catholic schools fomented conformist attitudes in the face of vertical structures of authority related to the political authoritarianism that sustained the revolutionary state."[77]

In later decades institutional medicine in Mexico continued to adopt an anti-abortion position. *El Informador* reported in 1969 that several presenters at the second Congress of the National Academy of Medicine decreed that "criminal abortion is condemnable, and the use of contraception is preferable in all cases."[78] As abortion moved more strongly into the public consciousness because of feminists' public advocacy, fewer physicians publicly supported the procedure. Where they did publish about it, they often adopted a condemnatory position. Sociologist Sandra Gonzáles Santos reports, for instance, that Guillero Corono Uhink, a Catholic doctor from the National Autonomous University of Mexico's medical school, published an article in 1964 in which he declared that women's use of contraceptives was immoral, and that their use, like abortion and the practice of giving children up for adoption, was "an alteration of the reproductive impulse."[79] A 1975 study of Mexico City doctors indicated that over 61 percent were opposed to providing abortions under any circumstances, although between 75 percent and 95 percent supported their performance if the pregnant woman faced a threat to her health, or if the fetus suffered from a grave medical defect.[80]

By the 1990s some institutions excluded medical instruction on the procedure, even in cases where it was lawful. Although some physicians continued to advocate for the need for safe, accessible abortions in the 1980s and 1990s, their voices were exceptional.[81] One 1992 sociological researcher interviewed medical personnel about their experiences providing surgical abortions to women or treating women experiencing complications of induced abortions. One of his subjects told him that physicians did not generally denounce patients to the police who appeared in hospitals because of complications from induced abortions. Nevertheless the Mexican Commission of the Defense and Promotion of Human Rights was at the time defending one woman denounced to a criminal court in these exact circumstances.[82] The interviewers' informants also declared that most physicians supported abortion, "but do not provide it out of fear of penalization."[83]

A 1997 study of ninety-six medical students from the Autonomous Metropolitan University-Xochimilco revealed that many students had limited knowledge of the legal status of abortion. They did not know, for instance, it was licit if childbirth threatened a woman's life.[84] Referring to several studies conducted between 2000 and 2010, Marta Lamas comments that many doctors objected to providing abortion because of their religious beliefs and others because they saw the women who sought them as "irresponsible."[85] One 2004 sociological study of thirty-four doctors working in public hospitals and clinics found that many both opposed providing abortions, even in cases of rape, and formed gendered judgements about their patients, including the assumption that their patients lived "promiscuously," worked as prostitutes, or were single mothers—"an expression that is never formulated without carrying with it a pejorative meaning."[86]

The impact of this shift in the availability of surgical abortions was somewhat lessened by the coincident rise of both contraception and pharmaceutical methods of inducing abortion. With increases in the availability of contraception beginning in the late 1970s, fewer women had to take recourse to abortion. The Gattermacher Institute reported in 2013 that seven out of ten married or cohabiting women of childbearing age used contraception, more than doubling the use of contraception since 1976, resulting in a decline of average family size from six children in the mid 1970s to just over two between 2006 and 2008.[87] The rise, since the mid-1980s, of women's use of pharmaceutical abortifacients has also reduced the need for the involvement of physicians in abortion since, in Mexico, such drugs can be acquired without prescriptions. A report from the Grupo Interdisciplinario para el Estudio de Aborto en México (Interdisciplinary Group for the Study of Abortion in Mexico, or GIEA) reported in 1976 that the ingestion of "potions and teas" was the most common method of provoking abortion in the country, especially in Indigenous communities.[88] Pharmaceutical abortions, like the ingestion of the anti-progesterone pill mifepristone (formerly known as RU-486), taken along with misoprostol, have been available over the counter in Mexican pharmacies since the mid 1980s.[89] In 2013 an extensive health professionals survey indicated that physicians provided less than one-quarter of all abortions recently obtained in Mexico.[90]

Feminist Reaction and Counterreaction, 1970s–90s

If little changed about the development of abortion at midcentury beyond its novel condemnation by institutional medicine, the last decades of the century witnessed the onset of significant changes to the law, feminist activism, and the Catholic counterreaction surrounding abortion. Adriana Ortiz-Ortega observes that by the mid-1970s, two principal factors rendered the Mexican state open to reforms of abortion law.[91] First, feminist organizing helped broaden the sector of the population receptive to the idea of abortion's permissibility. By the mid-1970s, feminist groups, which coalesced with the creation of the Coalición de Mujeres Feministas (Coalition of Feminist Women, or CMF), focused on defending victims of domestic violence, supporting victims of rape, and expanding access to abortion. In 1976 the Movimiento Nacional de Mujeres (National Movement of Women, or MNM) inaugurated the first Day of Abortion Liberalization and, from the late 1970s through the 1990s, staged marches, protests, and educational campaigns supporting greater reproductive freedom. In this period women's demands for "voluntary motherhood" became a core concept.[92] As Marta Lamas has discussed, the campaign for voluntary motherhood involved four key elements: the expansion of sexual education; greater access to contraception and, when necessary, abortion; and the cessation of women's nonvoluntary sterilization.[93]

From these campaigns the CMF presented bills for legalizing abortion to the Federal Assembly of Deputies in 1976, 1977, and 1979, but none were successful.[94] The 1979 initiative, titled the Bill for Voluntary Motherhood, was sponsored by newly elected congressional representatives of the Mexican Communist Party.[95] In the 1980s abortion seems to have become less of a central priority. Elizabeth Maier observes that grassroots feminist activists organizing women in poor urban neighborhoods prioritized matters other than abortion, such as securing "government welfare benefits, affordable housing, health care, and childcare services."[96] But in the early 1990s, various actors, led by activist Marta Lamas, united to form the country's most significant educational and political lobby group working on women's reproductive freedom: GIRE.[97]

Perhaps more important than feminist influences was the second factor Ortiz-Ortega identified as central to the state's changing attitudes to the legality of abortion. By the mid-1970s, the federal government had reversed its outlook on population management and natality. The dominant notion the Mexican government inherited from the previous century and continued to endorse throughout the 1960s was that Mexico was best served, socially and economically, by a program of indefinite population increase and thus the encouragement of natality under all circumstances. The postrevolutionary state adopted this policy in the wake of the terrible death toll of between 5 and 10 percent of the national population caused by the violence of the 1910 Revolution. The federal government's General Population Law of 1936 encouraged natural growth through marriage and reproduction and was accompanied by various public health measures aimed at promoting early childhood and familial well-being, as well as financial incentives for creating large families, and by the legal prohibition on the sale of contraceptives.[98]

However, beginning in the late 1950s, various actors at the state and federal levels of government began rejecting this idea and embracing the notion that Mexico's economy would be better served by population control rather than unfettered growth. In 1966 the government of Tabasco declared that demands for land were far outstripping the state's booming population, while, between 1956 and 1967, the states of Jalisco, Nuevo León, Tlaxcala, and Veracruz all avowed that the ongoing population increases they were facing would render them incapable of providing educational services to their inhabitants.[99] Another important force behind the state's reversal on the question of contraception, as Martha Liliana Espinosa Tavares and Stephanie Baker Opperman have detailed, were the efforts of American physician Edris Rice-Wray and her Mexican network of doctors, social workers, and scientists who discreetly established a family planning clinic in Mexico City in 1958.[100] By the early 1970s, both this network and the international foundations that supported its work had been lobbying the federal government on the imperative to change the country's population policy for over a decade.

Results of the 1970 census, ongoing findings by the state's Centro de Estudios Económicos y Demográficos (Center of Economic and Demographic Studies), and recognition of progressive physicians' support for controlling natality prompted a shift in population policy under the presidency of Luis Echeverría Álvarez (1970–76), whose administration orchestrated a dramatic reversal in the state's position on natality. In 1973 the state altered the Sanitary Code to allow for the sale of contraceptives and the following year issued two key statutes. As well as treating migration, the 1974 revision of the General Population Law obliged the state to provide free family planning to Mexican citizens and created the Consejo Nacional de Población (National Population Council) to administer it and to provide other family-oriented services. That same year the federal government also revised Article 4 of the National Constitution to assert both that "men and women are equal before the law," and that all people had the right to "decide in a free, responsible, and informed manner on the number and spacing of their children."[101] This article became a key foundation in the Supreme Court rulings on both the Federal District's 2007 first-trimester abortion depenalization and the 2021 ruling on Coahuila.[102]

In the mid-1970s, the Ministry of the Interior, in explaining the reasoning behind the 1974 General Population Law, acknowledged that an estimated five hundred thousand Mexican women underwent abortions annually, constituting between 15 and 20 percent of all pregnancies.[103] In this context the state organized the Interdisciplinary Group for the study of Abortion in Mexico to make recommendations about the matter and, in the late 1970s, persuaded various PRI governors to modify their states' penal codes to expand women's accessibility to abortion. Ortiz-Ortega describes the reforms occurring in a clientelist fashion typical of PRI political maneuvering: "Top officials in the López Portillo administration suggested to the President that it should be up to local deputies to advance decriminalization proposals. Upon presidential approval, top officials suggested to the governors in the states that a reform on abortion laws was necessary."[104] Political scientist Caroline Beer suggests that in the following decade, state governors could enact such changes because they enjoyed greater autonomy as the power of local governors increased in the era of successful political challenges to exclusive PRI rule.[105] State legislatures made changes to abortion law discreetly, to avoid provoking conservative attempts to block such changes. This also meant, of course, that those who might have benefited from this legislative leniency—pregnant women and their advocates—often remained ignorant of the changes.[106] As Ortiz-Ortega writes, "No mention was ever made of the modifications of the new penal codes by state officials; the new penal codes were not reprinted and the measures were not reported to the local or national press, nor disclosed to public hospitals, feminist groups or women."[107]

Ortiz-Ortega, however, may have exaggerated the secrecy; various contemporary newspapers did report on conservative groups' objections to the efforts to expand women's legal access to abortion. In 1978 the press reported that Fidel Velázquez, leader of the Confederation of Mexican Workers, announced that it was necessary for families to limit themselves to having only three children and stated: "I am not opposed to the legalization of abortion."[108] The following year the Mexican Democratic Party (PDM), through its state committee in Jalisco, declared itself opposed to that legislature's plans to expand abortion access.[109] The PDM asserted that abortion had never stopped being a crime, "among the most vile of these since it is committed against the most helpless of beings." The language used was telling: here the embryo or fetus had become a "being." By the early 1980s, the being became a child. A 1980 opinion piece published by physician Conrado Zuckerman, a former subsecretary of health who had served as president of the First Mexican Congress of Obstetrics and Gynecology in 1949, commented that he was working on a political campaign to defend children: "It is important to remember that the embryo, the fetus, in the maternal womb, is the antecedent, the precursor of the child, and that in reality, it can be considered like a child who lives in its appropriate medium, in its temporary place, which is indispensable for its development, before entering to the exterior environment of the world."[110] Although such changes in discourse are apparent in the 1980s, Caroline Beer notes that, despite the advocacy work of feminist groups, in political terms "abortion continued to be an issue of low salience throughout the 1990s, but then suddenly emerged as a central polarizing issue in the aftermath of the 2000 presidential elections."[111]

The secrecy surrounding changes in state codes respecting abortion in the 1980s makes it difficult to ascertain which states enacted which reforms to the 1931 Distrito Federal's penal code legislation at exactly what date. However, we do know that between the late 1980s and 2007, three broad levels of tolerance or persecution for abortion surfaced in different parts of the country: first, states with more progressive legislation (Distrito Federal, Hidalgo, Jalisco, Michoacán, Nayarit, Nuevo León, Tamaulipas, Tlaxcala, Yucatán, and Zacatecas) that did not penalize abortion if the mother's health was at stake or that recognized economic hardship as a justification for lawful abortion; second, intermediate states (Baja California Norte, Baja California Sur, Coahuila, Colima, Chihuahua, Chiapas, Estado de México, Morelos, Oaxaca, Puebla, Sonora,

Quintana Roo, Tabasco, and Veracruz) that did not criminalize abortion for the additional reasons of either genetic deformities in the fetus or because women had been impregnated in involuntary artificial insemination;[112] and, finally, those most conservative states (Aguascalientes, Campeche, Durango, San Luis Potosí, Sinaloa, and Tabasco) where abortion was only licit in those instances indicated in the 1871 penal code—to save the life of the mother, or when abortions were demonstrably accidental, or, as legalized in the 1931 addition, in instances of rape.[113] Guanajuato, in its 1978 reform of the penal code, went one step further and removed the clause allowing for an exemption to spare the life of the mother that had been in the state's codes in 1933 and 1956.[114]

There is a striking contradiction between both the historic (1871 and 1931) and 1980s exemptions for lawful abortion and the reasons real women provided to investigators as to why they sought abortion, at least in the mid-1970s. Since 1871 abortion had been legal in cases where pregnancy threatened women's lives, and since 1931 it was nonpunishable in cases of rape. However, neither condition addressed the most common reasons why women sought abortions. One 1971 report on over 2,600 abortions detailed that 0.25 percent of the women interviewed had sought abortions because of rape, and another 0.48 percent sought them because they worked as prostitutes. Meanwhile, over 50 percent of the women interviewed needed abortions because they already supported more children than they could afford, and another 27 percent faced poor economic circumstances.[115] A 1976 study by six Mexican researchers identified health as the reason for the abortions sought by their subjects; nor did any of the women interviewed identify their pregnancies as a result of rape, an extenuating circumstance that since 1931 the law had considered nonpunishable. Most women (79 percent) asserted that either an already excessive number of children or economic hardship were the most common reasons for seeking abortions, circumstances that by 1976 only the states of Yucatán, Chiapas, and Chihuahua declared rendered abortion noncriminal (or less criminal).[116] The issue of honor and shame—again, a mitigating factor the law had addressed since 1871—was a motivation for only a tiny portion of women, 6 percent, who sought abortions in 1976.[117] A second study, dating from 1990, revealed that inadequate economic resources continued to be the primary motive why most women aborted by that date and showed that 65 percent of women who had had abortions in Mexico were married, and 70 percent were mothers to numerous children.[118] The exceptions to penalization the law provided to women, derived from a penal code fashioned one century earlier, addressed the realities of very few Mexican women.

One other surprising aspect of the retention of nineteenth-century attitudes toward abortion in twentieth-century practice involves the endurance of the clauses relating to female sexual honor, the provisions referred to as the *honoris causa* clauses in the literature.[119] At the time of writing, just as in 1871, in six states of the federation (Jalisco, Nayarit, Oaxaca, Tamaulipas, Zacatecas, and Yucatán), the penalties for women convicted of abortion can be reduced if they are found to not have "bad reputations," have kept their pregnancies concealed, and have not been impregnated within marital unions.

The gendered assumptions that the producers and users of the 1871 penal code made are clear. What made abortion more or less heinous depended not on the on the status of the embryo or fetus whose development the act interrupted, but rather the impact of pregnancy on the honor of the pregnant woman, or, more importantly, on the honor of the men with whom she was associated. The code offered alleviations in the form of less severe sentences to women who had maintained a reputation of "buenas costumbres" who were convicted for abortion because it valued the maintenance of reputation above any other consideration. Women who had hidden their pregnancies were afforded similar protections because those who had not hidden them, the code assumed, had already lost their reputations for public virtue. Finally, those impregnated outside of marriage were allowed greater leniency because the code assumed that such women, if their pregnancies were acknowledged, would also suffer damage to their reputations.

These provisions may seem offensive or ludicrous to modern readers. But the 1871 abortion regulations were consistent with the logic of their time and with the prevalent concerns of the code and its framers. The centrality of public honor—its constant reenactment according to gendered codes of behavior and its contribution to social stability and the advancement of civilization—feature centrally in the 1871 code as a whole. Its sixth title dealt with "crimes against the order of families, public morality or good customs." The latter were defined as "all actions that in the public concept are deemed as contrary to modesty" and included such acts as hiding the birth of a child or falsely registering a birth before a justice, the corruption of minors, rape, adultery, pederasty, and bigamy.[120] All of these were considered offenses not to aggrieved parties (or, at least, not to them alone) but rather to the whole of civil society. The code's concern with public honor is also apparent in its handling of the circumstances that excluded defendants from criminal responsibility. Besides decrepitude, minority status, "mental derangement" and "complete drunkenness," defendants could avoid criminal responsibility when they had acted "in defense of their person, their honor, or their goods, or the person, honor, or goods of another."[121] Defending one's honor or the honor of another was as vital as defending one's own life. Historian Saydi Núñez Cetina points out that in the debates surrounding the possible changes to the penal code in 1929 and 1931, "the supposed benevolence or indulgence toward women who committed infanticide or practiced abortion depended greatly on their reputation and its maintenance within marriage, where it was protected because of its importance to the family and the nation."[122] Decades of researchers have shown that in the Porfiriato, public acknowledgment of women's sexual virtue lay at the foundation of female honor and, through it, familial and male honor. This remained the case through the next century; as Mariano Jiménez Huerta, a lawyer and legal scholar, commented in a 1959 article on the contemporary application of infanticide law in Mexico, the protection of honor that accounted for the crime was "honor spelled with a small h; that is, sexual honor."[123]

If the sexual honor clauses on abortion ruling are consistent with the Mexican legal framework of 1871, the anachronism of the application of the honoris causa clauses in abortion cases became clear to many who objected to them in the closing decades of the twentieth century. Privacy protection law does not permit archival research into criminal cases in Mexico after 1950, so few details are available in terms of courts' actual application of these clauses in legal cases in the past seventy years.[124] However, various public sources indicate that these elements of many states' abortion laws form an important component of challenges to abortion's penalization. As late as 1959 it did not occur to lawyer Jiménez Huerta that the premise of differently sentencing defendants according to their embodiment of "good" or "bad" reputations might merit a legal interrogation; his article focused instead on such matters as whether only the blood relatives of the pregnant woman, and not those of the man who had impregnated her, should be given access to the protections the law afforded, since, as he noted, the evaluation of honor would not affect "the family of the father of a child that a woman estranged from them."[125] Another professor of law, Francisco Pavon Vasconcelos, wrote in a 1959 article that the honoris causa clauses in the code made a great deal of sense, so long as it was understood that "the bad reputation (*mala fama*) that the Code refers to is <u>sexual</u> *mala fama*."[126] Concern over maintaining *buena fama* may not describe the preoccupations of women in the late twentieth and early twenty-first century, but as discussed, such concerns did and do continue to inform assumptions the medical profession made about them.

In recent decades activists, legislators, and lawyers challenging Mexico's abortion laws presented reasoned objections to the logical and legal flaws in the honoris causa clauses. One such argument, presented by Senator Javier Orozco Gómez in 2011, sought to reform the Federal District code's treatment of abortion on the basis of the illogic of the clauses. As his brief demanded, in the context of a judicial hearing, such considerations are not only ridiculous, but also unprovable: "How can one prove that a woman is not of ill repute or that she tried to hide her pregnancy? On what basis is the judge to decide whether or not a woman is of ill repute?"[127] In its upholding of Mexico City's 2007 decriminalization of first-trimester abortions, justices also referred to the inappropriateness of the moral evaluations of women these clauses constructed.[128]

One of the other most curious and least discussed recent changes to abortion law in Mexico involves the depenalization of abortions in cases of involuntary artificial insemination. President Miguel de la Madrid (1982–88) first included this initiative, along with the decriminalization of abortion in cases of extreme poverty and fetal deformation, when he prompted Attorney General García Sergio Ramírez to introduce a proposal to the National Chamber of Deputies in 1983.[129] Feminists and Catholic factions in the house clashed over the proposal, and as a compromise, the chamber accepted only one of the three parts of the policy. As political scientist Linda Stevenson observes, the portion they elected to adopt was the one that "no one was quite sure how to interpret—pregnancies caused by unwanted artificial insemination."[130] De la Madrid's proposal may have been the origin for those state codes that subsequently decriminalized abortions in such instances. The following year Article 466 of the General Law of Health was also amended to penalize those who impregnated women without their consent via artificial insemination.[131]

Sociologist Eduardo Barraza considers that in contemplating how to implement Article 466, some states criminalized nonconsensual artificial insemination resulting in pregnancies, while others criminalized those that resulted in abortions.

As early as 1994, both the states of Colima and Querétaro included amendments in their state codes decriminalizing abortion in cases of pregnancies resulting from involuntary artificial insemination.[132] More recently this exemption was added by another ten states.[133] However, even though legal scholars, historians, political scientists, and feminist activists all frequently describe this legal change, no existent scholarship explains why and when states amended their codes in this way. Perhaps they did it because it was a way to signal liberalization, without actually having to enact liberalization, since instances of abortions in such conditions, if they did occur, occurred without public acknowledgment. Another explanation for the inclusion of this clause is that it was related to the science (and business) of fertility research in which Mexican women participated with and without full consent beginning in the 1980s. The feminist publication *Fem* began publishing articles discussing in vitro fertilization (IVF) in Mexico in the late 1980s, and one 1992 article in the journal by Mercedes Fereirra discussed the legal problems involved in transplanting "an unwanted embryo to a voluntary carrier as an alternative to abortion," a medical procedure evidently practiced at the time.[134]

In her research on assisted reproduction in Mexico, Sandra Gonzáles-Santos notes that IVF practices raised moral dilemmas in Mexico in the 1980s because of the ethics of disposing of fertilized eggs that were not transferred into women's bodies.[135] In publications from the mid-1990s, the anti-abortion group ProVida denounced artificial insemination (whether consensual or not). When two representatives to Nuevo León's legislature proposed a reform of the state's abortion law in 1995, Jorge Serrano Limón, president of the ProVida, declared that "assisted reproduction" worked against human life, since artificial insemination required "the freezing of many children, of whom many die, and others remain frozen."[136]

Recent evidence documents that American firms have used Mexican women as subjects for fertility experimentation, including in instances involving the termination of multiple fertilized embryos. In 2020 an American company called CooperGenomics acknowledged its use of eighty-one Mexican women in the state of Nayarit as subjects in fertility research. The women received hormone injections, were inseminated "naturally" by sperm, and had their fertilized embryos "flushed" for further study.[137] Laurie Zoloth, a University of Chicago bioethicist, charged CooperGenomics with "ethics dumping," referring to state and private practices of conducting research using unethical practices which are exported from higher to lower-income settings. It is possible, then, that Mexican women used in research conducted by a Mexican or American fertility firm would have been implicated by state abortion laws, and that the facilities conducting such research sought legal exemption for the work. The Distrito Federal amended its penal code in 2002 to declare that parties would be imprisoned to between three and six years convicted for using "eggs or sperm for ends different form those authorized by their donors."[138] In 2012 the state of Puebla included a similar revision to its code to castigate those who, "without previous informed consent, undertake the extraction of eggs, artificial insemination, or the transfer of embryos to a woman older than eighteen years."[139]

As Serrano Limón's comments demonstrate, Catholic organizations have been, since the 1980s, vocal opponents of both enhanced fertility practices and abortion. At the close of the twentieth century, the Catholic Church, allied with Christian Evangelicals, became the strongest champion of the entrenchment or augmentation of penalization for abortion in Mexico, including in cases involving artificial insemination. Catholic opposition to abortion, as discussed, was not particularly powerful in Mexico until this era. Nor did lobbying by Catholic groups have notable impact on legislative changes before 2000, despite the fact that the papacy sporadically issued directives treating abortion in the late twentieth century. In 1968 Pope Paul VI issued an encyclical *Humanae Vitae*, reasserting the church's opposition to artificial contraception, and in 1977 Guadalajara's Catholic daily, *El Informador*, reported that Paul had denounced those countries, including Great Britain and the United States, that had recently legalized abortion.[140] In 1995 John Paul II published *Evangelium Vitae*, condemning abortion and euthanasia. Five years earlier John Paul had traveled to Mexico and in the city of Chihuahua delivered a speech conveying the same message.[141]

But rather than Vatican directives serving as the most powerful stimuli for Catholic organizers, opposition to vocal feminist pro-choice demonstrations and lobbying proved their strongest inducement. In 1976, the year the MNM inaugurated the first Day of Abortion Liberalization, the office of the archbishop of Guadalajara issued a publication, as Guadalajara's Catholic newspaper the *Informador* reported, declaring that no circumstances justified provoking abortions, including the health of the mother, her economic realities, or the medical prognosis of the fetus.[142] In 1978, when feminist groups began petitioning the National Assembly to push for abortion's depenalization, the archbishop of Mexico helped found the local chapter of the international pro-life group ProVida. Subsequently, such organizations as ProVida and Vida y Familia lobbied state and federal representatives of the PAN to sponsor bills guaranteeing the life of the unborn. Lawyer Luis de la Barreda Solorzano observes that the impetus motivating the Episcopal Mexican Conference to issue a pastoral message, "Abortion and Depenalization," in 1983 was not a new directive on abortion originating in the Vatican but, rather, the liberalizing reforms President Miguel de la Madrid's attorney general introduced into the Chamber of Deputies that year.[143]

One reason for the church's inability to intervene in Mexico's political life before the close of the twentieth century was a set of directives mandated by Article 130 of the 1917 Constitution. This article, which President Carlos Salinas revoked in 1992, had prevented the recognition of the church as a legal entity and restricted it from intervening in political matters, while also denying the clergy from exercising political rights. Through much of the twentieth century, the Catholic Church did not attempt to intervene in the legal regulation of reproduction. Rather, the church's constitutional exclusion from participating in affairs of the state meant, according to demographer Gustavo Cabrera, that it had "developed great tolerance regarding the contraceptive practices of its congregation."[144]

Catholic organizations' political opposition to abortion intensified in the course of the 1980s, but especially in the 1990s, when its organizing helped defeat legislative efforts to liberalize abortion in the state of Chiapas in 1990 and in the National Assembly of Deputies in 1991. Such organizing also succeeded in inducing the legislature of Chihuahua to amend that state's constitution in 1994 with language affirming that life begins at conception. Nuevo León tried but failed to pass a similar amendment in 1999. The role of Catholic lobbying, including among medial professionals, was crystallized in the 1999 "Paulina" case, involving Paulina del Carmen Ramírez Jacinto, a fourteen-year-old raped and impregnated in a home invasion in Mexicali, Baja California del Norte. Although the state's attorney general had ruled that Ramírez had the legal right to an abortion, no physician at the city's general hospital would agree, on moral grounds, to perform the procedure. Anti-abortion representatives assailed Ramírez when she was hospitalized after the rape to dissuade her from pursuing an abortion by showing her a U.S.-produced anti-abortion film, *The Silent Scream* (1984).[145] The state governor ultimately refused to allow the procedure to be carried out, and Ramírez was forced to carry the pregnancy to term.

The presence of this American film in the hands of Mexican anti-abortion activists in a Mexicali hospital room in 1999 was no coincidence. Transnational anti-abortion groups, both Protestant Evangelical and Catholic, mainly from the United States but also from western Europe, had targeted Mexico and Central America in missionary campaigns since the 1980s through such organizations as the World Congress of Families and Human Life International.[146] Adherents to Evangelical churches in Mexico and elsewhere in Latin America express a much more hard-line stance on abortion than does the region's Catholic-identifying population.[147]

Two further conflicts over abortion legislation absorbed Mexico in 1999 and 2000. In the former the PAN-controlled state legislature of Guanajuato attempted to pass a legislative change in order to penalize abortion in all instances, including rape. However, in this case, significant popular mobilization against the initiative convinced the governor to veto the bill. In Mexico City in 2000, propelled by the example of the Paulina case, the municipal assembly passed a set of reforms, subsequently referred to as the "Ley Robles" (Robles law), named after the law's champion, feminist academic and Democratic Revolutionary Party mayor Rosario Robles. These reforms expanded the instances in which women could lawfully abort to include not only accidental causes and rape (permitted in the 1931 code) but also threats to the pregnant woman's health, malformations of the fetus, and pregnancies caused by involuntary artificial insemination.

One of the oddities of the Robles law was that it was controversial, even though some of the exceptions it introduced had been quietly depenalized in various states years, and in some instances decades, earlier. Three years before the Robles law, for example, Chihuahua's criminal code had depenalized abortion in cases of involuntary artificial insemination, while Puebla had decriminalized abortion in cases of "grave eugenic factors" (meaning fetal nonviability) as early as 1986 (and Sonora, as mentioned, had done so in 1940).[148] After the Federal District passed these exemptions, which withstood a challenge before the nation's Supreme Court in 2002, many other states followed suit. The Robles law was the first instance in which the Supreme Court issued an abortion ruling. In its decision, while the court declared that fetal life should be protected from the moment of conception, it also validated the legal foundations for interrupting pregnancy in its expression of the seemingly contradictory idea, as Marta Lamas describes it, that there were pretexts upon which it was not illegal to abort, "but that these were compatible with the notion of life from the moment of conception."[149] The SCJN's ruling on the Robles law was not an unmediated pro-choice victory: it did not challenge the fundamental pro-life position on the sanctity of human life created at the moment of conception, and as legal scholar Alejandro Madrazo observes, the court's majority opinion spent seventy paragraphs establishing the constitutional protection of the fetus's right to life and "only one paragraph, near the end, considering the woman's plight, and then only in cases of severe fetal malformations."[150]

Conclusion

Until its closing decade, when both the Supreme Court and state legislatures became enmeshed in fraught decisions about abortion law, inertia characterized abortion's legal dimensions across the twentieth century. The text and the rationale of the crime's regulation, first articulated in the modern era in the Federal District's 1871 penal code, went largely unchanged in the country for over a century, with the significant exception of the 1931 penal code's depenalization of abortion in cases of rape. Inertia also characterized the fact of the nonsensical longevity of the 1871 code's honoris causa clauses. Their articulation of the mitigating circumstances in which women of buena fama, those who hid pregnancies, and those impregnated in extramarital unions might receive lighter punishments than others convicted for abortion were consistent with dominant gendered assumptions of the late nineteenth century, but seem ludicrous a century later, despite the fact that in recent decades medical professionals have continued to apply these same gendered assumptions to their assessments of patients seeking abortions under their care.

The Catholic Church, long understood as the source of vocal opposition to abortion in Mexico, in fact played a fairly insignificant role in shaping abortion's twentieth-century trajectory, except in the final decade of the century, when Catholic lay organizations emerged as prominent lobbyists and political actors. The one surprising realm in which Catholic formulations are evident much earlier in twentieth-century abortion debates was, at midcentury, when growing numbers of professional medical associations adopted a novel anti-abortion position. Doctors who articulated this position, in professional meetings and published papers, linked their objections explicitly to Catholic considerations. But the church itself, prohibited until 1992 from public political discourse, limited its public interventions on the issue.

How much did feminist groups influence the development of twentieth-century abortion legislation? Caroline Beer writes that feminist groups had little dramatic impact on mobilizing for changes to abortion law in the 1970s and 1980s, particularly outside of Mexico City. However, many other writers, including Marta Lamas, see feminist advocacy as imperative to creating the context for legislative and judicial change.[151] Rather than attempting to measure the impact of pro-choice groups on the passage of particular laws or on the formulation of specific judicial rulings, it may be more revealing to consider the impact of the past four decades of feminist organizing and thinking in Mexico in broader terms. We might consider, for instance, how feminist scholarship, political organizing, and popular campaigning contributed to changing public thinking at the more basic level of the acceptance of women's right to self-determination. Elizabeth Maier observes that although feminism was "never a mass movement in Mexico," it was nevertheless influential: "The current debate on abortion has highlighted the degree to which feminist discourse has been adopted over the years by a wide range of intellectuals and opinion makers unwaveringly defending a free-choice, public health perspective."[152]

The feminist notion that women are people and as such, possess the right to make fundamental decisions about their bodies, economic lives, and families has affected the Mexican public in broad and substantial ways, including on the issue of abortion. Public opinion surveys conducted in the 1990s and 2000s revealed that, strong popular "Catholic values" notwithstanding, a majority of the country's male and female population believe women should have the right to decide what happens to their own bodies. Two-thirds of respondents in one 1991 poll conducted by the Instituto Mexicano de Investigación en Familia y Población (Mexican Institute of Research on Family and Population, or IMIFP) in Mexico City and Chiapas agreed that the pregnant woman herself should have the exclusive right to decide whether or not to induce an abortion.[153] In a second IMIFP and Gallup poll from 1992, three-quarters of respondents asserted that the decision to abort should be made by the pregnant woman or the couple that had created the pregnancy but not the government or the church.[154] By 2009 74 percent of over nine hundred adults in Mexico City surveyed supported Mexico City's legalization of first-trimester abortions.[155] The SCJN's 2021 decriminalization of abortion in Mexico appears radically progressive when juxtaposed with the more conservative direction the U.S. Supreme Court is moving on the question of abortion, but in fact it is in line not only with the laws and judiciaries of other American and European countries but also the values of a majority of Mexico's national population.

CONCLUSION

By the late twentieth century, the broader Mexican public held a more permissive attitude toward abortion than did contemporaneous medical personnel. Of course, it is hard to know for certain whether this attitude reflected a way of thinking that was unique to the last decades of the twentieth century, as no one was polling the Mexican public on the matter in the 1950s, let alone in the 1850s. From 1588 to 1869, papal decrees and viceregal religious literature produced in or for the inhabitants of New Spain condemned abortion, and secular law decreed it criminal and harshly punishable. Nevertheless, neither members of the public, state representatives, nor sacred authorities prioritized abortion as a moral or social issue of great import in Mexico though the viceregal era and up until the closing decades of the nineteenth century. This was the case even though, throughout this period and long after it, women acquired medicinal knowledge and treatments from midwives, family members, neighbors, boticarios, and merchants about plant-based abortifacients and used these as effective means to control reproduction.

Alongside this evidence of women's use of such methods to induce medicinal abortions, this book's examination of the history of surgical abortion in Mexico reveals that, rather than standing as the historic patriarchal opponents of access to abortion, many individual physicians (and the professional organizations to which they belonged) researched, published about, and performed surgical abortions during the period between roughly 1880 and 1950. Although differences of opinion regarding the morality of abortion existed within the profession, many doctors defended their legal right to perform, and their patients' right to access, abortions when they deemed these necessary. Many doctors focused on improving the techniques used to perform such procedures safely and effectively. Most doctors deemed abortions necessary when pregnancy or childbirth threatened women's lives and considered it not only lawful but also ethical in cases of rape; others thought abortion permissible when pregnancy threatened women's health. Smaller numbers supported abortion when women lacked the economic means to care for their offspring. In the later twentieth century, some physicians supported abortion when the products of conception gave indication of severe genetic conditions.

In the mid-twentieth century, however, a number of prominent spokespeople for the medical profession and several medical organizations reversed their former support for doctors' performance of abortion, even in those cases permitted by law. The sources examined here give some indication that newly asserted moral convictions of doctors explained this shift, but the changes may also relate to the broader history of the state's political and institutional relationship to the profession. The state after 1940 became increasingly more conservative at the same time as the medical profession experienced decreased autonomy from governmental regulation. The decade was also typified by a movement of state and social gender conservatism in comparison to the comparative radicalism of the 1930s, when thousands of women had been active in such political organizations as Acción Femenina (Feminine Action), and when the country hosted three national congresses of Women's Workers and Peasants.[1] In contrast the most significant post–World War II women's political organization in Mexico, the Unión Nacional de Mujeres, denounced even the use of birth control, let alone abortion.[2] Another powerful women's organization of the 1950s, Acción Católica, focused on the corrupting influence that "modernity" had wrought on Mexicans' sexual proclivities.[3] In her research Nichole Sanders points to this shift, highlighting the telling portrayal of Mexican women's roles that "the laws of the Revolution" had "pledged to conserve," as President Miguel Alemán proclaimed in 1946. Women had been and should remain "incomparable mothers, sacrificing and diligent wives, loyal sisters and modest daughters."[4]

Martha Santillán Esqueda, who writes about abortion history in the 1930s–50s, has studied the scandalous case, widely condemned in contemporary newspapers in the capital city, of physician González de la Vega, arrested in 1941 at his clinic along with twenty of his patients, for performing an alleged twenty to thirty abortions a day.[5] Santillán comments that contemporary reporting lay the blame for his patients' demand for abortion at the door of "moderniza-tion." As one columnist asserted, de la Vega's patients had misunderstood the idea of modernization in supposing that it implied "spurning the home and the institution of marriage" and replacing these with "a faith in contraception and divorce."[6] Historians have traced the shift to the political right of those presidents—Manuel Ávila Camacho (1940–46) and Miguel Alemán Valdés (1946–52)—in such matters as economic redistribution, agrarian reform, and press censorship. As one contemporary journalist, Carlos Denegri, observed, with the assumption of the Alemán presidency, "the Revolution has gotten off its horse and into a Cadillac."[7]

Susie Porter points out that the prominent lawyer and sociologist José Itur-riaga crystallized this more socially conservative position in his prominent 1951 text, *La estructura social y cultural de México*.[8] Iturriaga, while celebrating the growth of Mexico's middle class, also warned of broad transformations that were infecting Mexican society, particularly the Mexican family. Families were smaller, and divorce had skyrocketed between the mid-1930s and mid-1940s. The main culprit for Iturriaga, Porter observes, were women who, in literally earning their independence, no longer needed to stay in unsatisfying marriages.[9]

Perhaps influenced by this broad societal move embracing gender conser-vatism, articles and speeches by doctors, and surveys of and interviews with health-care professionals in the second half of the twentieth century docu-ment the inclination toward the condemnation of abortion within professional medical circles in the second half of the twentieth century. Medical students were not well informed on the legal foundations for abortion, nor were they consistently instructed on medical procedures involved in its performance. In fact physicians' understanding that inducing the interruption of a pregnancy constituted "homicide" made them more disposed to denouncing suspected clandestine abortions and to block access to the procedure, even in cases where the law permitted it, as occurred in case of the Mexicali youth Paulina Ramírez Jacinto in 1999. The SCJN decision of September 2021 overthrowing Article 10 of the 2018 Ley General de Salud becomes particularly significant in light of this historic trend. The court's ruling overturned the right of medical workers' con-scientious objection to the provision of health-care services involving abortion indicates that widespread existence of medical opposition to abortion existed in Mexico at the time of the ruling. The court declared these unconstitutional infringements on pregnant persons' rights to adequate medical care.

It is possible that the broader public was never strongly opposed to abortion, and that opposition was always most strongly concentrated—at least after 1950—in the medical establishment and among Catholic-oriented academics, politicians, and legislators. The low numbers of denunciations for the crime during the viceregal period and the first five decades after independence, as well as medical professionals' pre-1950s endorsement of the procedure, suggest that abortion was rather more popularly accepted than prohibited in these earlier eras than was the case between the mid-1950s and late 1980s. But both changes in physicians' attitudes toward the procedure (as discussed in chapter 3) and some indications of broader popular attitudes from after 1950 reveal that anti-abortion positions became more popular in this era. One 1975 survey of 411 Mexico City women documented a more pronounced anti-abortion attitude at that time than existed by the late 1990s. In the 1975 study, over 61 percent of the respondents opposed abortion on demand, and only 38 percent agreed it should be allowable in cases of rape.[10] There is some evidence, then, of decreased support for abortion from the 1950s to the mid-1970s, which then shifted back to a period of greater receptiveness to abortion, intensifying in the past decade. Successful politicization and educational campaigns by feminist activists likely contributed to this change.

Along with the absence of colonial and early republican zealousness in policing and prosecuting the crime of abortion, its history in the viceregal and early republican eras also contrasts with our own in terms of the absence in these earlier periods of a significant discourse about the sanctity of human life and the inherent value of newborn babies or unborn fetuses. Although these ideas are central to the anti-abortion position today, such ideas rarely entered the conversation about abortion in the seventeenth, eighteenth, and nineteenth centuries. In the 1930s the postrevolutionary state, addressing the dramatic depopulation of the country in the wake of a ten-year civil war, was the first to embrace the idea of child welfare in its adoption of an imperative to support child and mother welfare though state-funded and eugenics-influenced puericulture programs. However, even these efforts made few connections to the broader legal, philosophical, or spiritual question of the inherent value of human life, or the inherent rights of unborn embryos or fetuses. Such ideas were simply not part of the discussion. The discourse of fetal humanity did not emerge in Mexico, as is the case internationally, until the last decades of the twentieth century, and it emerged not in response to new concerns about human rights or the inherent value of human life, but rather in direct response to the heightened energy of feminist groups who began pushing in this period for the expansion of women's control over reproduction and other initiatives crucial to women's self-determination.

Feminist activism and education did not have a profound influence on abortion law until the twenty-first century, first with the capital's passage of the Robles law in 2000, with the legal changes introduced in 2007, and the Supreme Court ruling on these the following year, but especially with the SCJN's 2021 decision. Legal scholars trace the transformative feminist influence on recent judicial decisions in the logic underpinning the SCJN's decisions in the Robles law case, and in its assessment of the 2007 Distrito Federal legislative change legalizing first-trimester abortion. Reva Siegel assesses how recent judicial decisions in Mexico and elsewhere have evolved from an earlier perspective of abortion in which the rights of one party (the fetus) were assessed against those of a second (the pregnant person). Siegel examines how feminist organizing increasingly influenced courts "to acknowledge, accommodate, and even respect women's agency in abortion—most strikingly on the constitutional ground that this provides a more expansive way to protect the right to life of the unborn."[11] Referring to the European context, Siegel comments that judicial decisions are more frequently finding in favor of permitting women (rather than physicians, husbands, or the state) to decide whether or not to abort "on the constitutional ground that it is the best way to protect unborn life."[12] Thus 2010 Spanish legislation permitting first-trimester abortion asserts that "protecting prenatal life is more effective through policies to support pregnant women and maternity."[13] Alejandro Madrazo sees a similar shift to focusing primarily on the pregnant person, rather than the unborn fetus, as the central protagonist of abortion law in the Supreme Court's 2008 decision upholding the Distrito Federal's decriminalization of first trimester abortion.

My purpose in writing this book has been to highlight the differences between what past populations in Mexico thought or did or wrote about abortion and what they think and say about it now. I think this is an important objective, and in pursuing it, I seek to address current political conversations. One of the powerful ways the past shapes the present is that it operates, rhetorically, as a great legitimizer. When we believe things were done in a particular way or for particular purposes in the past, we often assume there was an inherent value to this precedent, and we accept it as a defense against change. Part of the job of a historian is to uncover and dismantle those moments when our assumptions about the practices of the past, or the reasons why they occurred, are inaccurate. Sometimes, especially on fraught political topics like abortion, our projections about the past speak most clearly about our present convictions and greatly distort past realities because we are not actually trying to see them.

Cultural critic Raymond Williams writes about this tendency in his book *The Country and the City*, in what he calls the effect of the "nostalgic escalator." There he describes how members of every generation stand on an imaginary escalator surveying the past as it extends below them, bemoaning that theirs is the last to generation have experienced virtuous, authentic lives (in Williams's context, authentically virtuous rural lives).[14] He also points out that the moment of moral authenticity is often located in the period of the author's own childhood, hence the particularly nostalgic view the escalator provides to the past.

I think that on the question of abortion, in my own country of Canada, as in those countries south of mine—the United States and Mexico—many ride the nostalgic escalator to create distorted ideas about abortion practices and attitudes in the past. Riders, whether pro-choice or anti-abortion, assume that the church, which is a linchpin of abortion opposition in our own day, headed opposition to abortion in the past. It did not. They assume that greater numbers of women will resort to abortion to control their fertility if it is legalized, and that legalization is an initiative new to our day. In fact some forms of abortion have been decriminalized in Mexico since 1871, others since 1931. Furthermore, women in Mexico have possessed the means to control their fertility through abortion among other means for centuries, and they will use these means whether the state prohibits or condones them. The one thing that will change in response to legalization, however, is women's willingness to seek state-sponsored medical aid for abortion-related care when they require it.

NOTES

Introduction

1. Madrazo, "Evolution of Mexico City's Abortion Laws," 267.
2. Madrazo, "Evolution of Mexico City's Abortion Laws," 267.
3. As Singer, *Lawful Sins*, 3, observes, only Cuba and Guyana treated voluntary abortion as lawful in 2007.
4. "Decreto por el que se reforma el Código Penal." Unless otherwise indicated, all translations from Spanish to English in this book are mine.
5. Madrazo, "Evolution of Mexico City's Abortion Laws," 269.
6. Secretaría de Salud, "Norma Oficial Mexicana NOM-046-SSA2-2005."
7. Inter-American Commission on Human Rights, "Report No. 21/7, Petition 161-02."
8. Article 196 of the state penal code mandated this prison sentence, Article 198 impeded women from seeking medical assistance for abortion, and Article 199 restricted lawful abortions sought in cases of rape to those occurring in the trimester of pregnancy.
9. Suprema Corte de Justicia de la Nación, "Suprema Corte declara inconstitucional la criminalización total del aborto."
10. At the time of writing, for instance, a member of Querétaro's state legislature had just introduced a bill to decriminalize abortion in that state, currently the most conservative one in the country in terms of abortion access.
11. Suprema Corte de Justicia de la Nación, "Mexican Supreme Court."
12. Both the *New York Times* and the *New Yorker* reported in 2022 about the Mexican activist group Las Libres, who sought to arrange for the distribution of the abortifacient misoprostol from Mexico (available without prescription) across the border. See Brent MacDonald, Paula Mónaco Felipe, Caroline Kim, Souleyman Messalti, and Miguel Tovar, "Mexican Activists Answer Calls for Abortion Pills in the U.S.," *New York Times*, July 15, 2022, https://www.nytimes.com/2022/07/15/world/americas/abortion-pills-mexico-us.html; and Stephania Taladrid, "The Post-Roe Abortion Underground," *New Yorker*, October 17, 2022,

https://www.newyorker.com/magazine/2022/10/17/the-post-roe-abortion-underground. Singer, *Lawful Sins*, 6, also notes that in the decades before the Supreme Court ruling *Roe v. Wade* (1973), hundreds of American women "traveled South to procure abortions from underground Mexican providers."

13. Tuman, Roth-Johnson, and Jelen, "Conscience and Context," 101.

14. GIRE (Grupo de Información en Reproducción Elegida), or the Reproductive Choice Educational Collective, reports that 4,246 abortions were denounced between 2007 and 2016, resulting in 98 convictions. GIRE, *Maternidad o castigo*, 60, 64.

15. Singer, *Lawful Sins*, 36.

16. There is an enormous literature on honor and gender in colonial and nineteenth-century Mexico. Key works include Lavrin, "Introduction," 10–14; Twinam, *Public Lives, Private Secrets*; Lipsett-Rivera, *Gender and the Negotiation of Daily Life*; and Sloan, *Runaway Daughters*.

17. Archivo Histórico Judicial de Oaxaca (hereafter AHJO), Teposcolula, Criminal, leg. 66, exp. 1, cuaderno 1, fol. 54v.

18. Erviti, *El aborto entre mujeres*, 269 (emphasis in the original).

19. Barreda Solórzano, *El delito de aborto*, 30.

20. Sahagún, *Historia general*, 2:606–7.

21. Schiebinger, *Plants and Empire*, 111.

22. This was the sentence for Bernarda Sulú, a midwife from Chochulá, Yucatán, sentenced in 1849 for supplying medicines to two women who aborted. Sulú, however, managed to flee from custody and never served her sentence.

23. Herrasti, "Algunos Mitos y Realidades."

24. Cantú et al., "Actitud del médico ante el aborto," 283.

25. Gonzáles de León Aguirre and Salinas Urbina, "Los médicos en formación," 227–36.

26. Shelton, "Infanticidio y disciplina," 293.

27. Juárez et al., "Estimates of Induced Abortion in Mexico," 158–68.

28. GIRE, *Omission and Indifference*, 17.

1. 1519–1870

1. Archivo General de la Nación, México (hereafter AGNM), Indiferente Virreinal, caja 6271, exp. 26, fols. 22, 23v.

2. This chapter draws from several of my earlier publications: *Reproduction and Its Discontents in Mexico*, 77–103; "Maternity and Morality," 299–319; and "Medicine, Midwifery, and the Law," 61–92. The chapter synthesizes the primary source materials used in all three publications and adds new material treating the history of state and church prohibition (and permissiveness) of abortion as well as material gauging abortion's popular perception in Mexico gleaned from news and periodical publications.

3. Archivo General del Estado de Yucatán (hereafter AGEY), Justicia, Penal, caja 101, vol. 101, exp. 6.

4. AGNM, Tribunal Superior de Justicia del Distrito Federal (hereafter TSJDF), caja 357. This same slippage occurs in the 1863 trial of Pastoral Qunital in Mérida, whose case is described on the title page as involving "voluntary abortion" but whose judges later referred to her crime as "infanticide." AGEY, Justicia, Penal, caja 122, vol. 122, exp. 32.

5. The interpermeability of perceptions of abortion and infanticide did not terminate in the nineteenth century. "Una famula mato al fruto de sus amores," *El Nacional*, July 8, 1932, 1, a news story published in a daily in the Mexican capital, reported on a woman who "provoked an abortion" and (referring to the same crime) committed an "infanticide."

6. See, for example, this claim asserted by Vida Humana Internacional (Human Life International), "La doctrina de la Iglesia en contra de la aborto [*sic*] es inmutable," May 9, 2018, https://vidahumana.org/la-doctrina-de-la-iglesia-en-contra-de-la-aborto-es-inmutable/.

7. This genealogy is replicated in numerous pro-life texts, including in a text by the recently disgraced Luis Francisco Serrano Limón, brother of José Serrano Limón (also recently disgraced), who headed ProVida Mexico from 1987 to 2001. See Serrano Limón, *Aborto en México: ¿Crisis o Solución?*, 17–21. The same intellectual lineage appears in the U.S. Conference of Catholic Bishops, "Respect for Unborn Human Life: The Church's Constant Teaching," accessed December 8, 2023, https://www.newadvent.org/cathen/01645a.htm.

8. Aristotle, *On the Generation of Animals*, book 2, chapter 1.

9. Aristotle, *On the Generation of Animals*, book 2, chapter 3.

10. Aristotle, *History of Animals*, book 7, part 3.

11. Aristotle, *History of Animals*, book 7, part 3.

12. Van Dyke, "Review."

13. Aristotle, *Politica*, book 7, chapter 16, in *Basic Works*, 1302 (emphasis in the original).

14. Noonan, "Abortion and the Catholic Church," 110.

15. Christopoulos, *Abortion in Early Modern Italy*, 140–49.

16. Christopoulos, *Abortion in Early Modern Italy*, 148.

17. *Concilio III Provincial Mexicano*, 405.

18. University of Arizona Library Special Collections, "Casos reservados sinodales en la Diócesis de México."

19. University of Arizona Library Special Collections, "Casos reservados sinodales en la Diócesis de México," 130.

20. Ximeno, *Opúsculo sobre los catorce casos reservados*, 27–28.

21. Ximeno, *Opúsculo sobre los catorce casos reservados*, 28.

22. Lumbier, *Noticia de las sesenta y cinco proposiciones nuevamente condenadas*.

23. Catholic Church, *A Decree Made at Rome* (capitalization in the original).

24. Enciso Rojas, "Mal parir," 97.

25. O'Brien, *Surgery and Salvation*, chapter 1.

26. Encisco Rojas, "Mal parir," 106. O'Brien notes in "Many Meanings of *Aborto*," 954, that Pius's 1854 proclamation was preceded in 1708 by Pope Clement's addition of the feast of Immaculate Conception to the liturgical calendar, which he deemed should be celebrated nine months before Mary's birth.

27. O'Brien, "Many Meanings of *Aborto*," 953. Her position is shared by many others, including Maier, "La disputa sobre el aborto en México," 20. News articles frequently characterize *Apostolicae Sedis* as a powerful anti-abortion declaration. See, for instance, Patsy McGarry, "Catholic Church Teaching on Abortion Dates from 1869," *Irish Times*, July 1, 2013, https://www.irishtimes.com/news/social-affairs/religion-and-beliefs/catholic-church-teaching-on-abortion-dates-from-1869-1.1449517.

28. I am grateful to Dylan Wilkerson for translating the bull into English for me. He worked from the following original Latin version of the text: Pius Episcopus Servorum Dei ad Perpetuam Re Momoriam, "Constitutio SS. D. N. PII PP. IX," 536–44.

29. One article, "Orden circular contra la propaganda Protestante," *La voz de México*, December 10, 1885, 2–3, commented instead on "Protestant propaganda." Another, "Del Vaticano: De las sectas de los francmasones," *El Tiempo*, August 26, 1884, discussed freemasonry. Contemporary discussions of other papal decrees treating matters far removed from abortion, including Leo XIII's encyclical, *Rerum Novarum*, which took up the question of the rights and responsibilities of capital and labor, garnered far more contemporary press coverage than did *Apostolicae Sedis*.

30. Catholic Church, *Catecismo para uso de los párrocos*, 229.

31. De Alva, *Guide to Confession Large and Small*, 102. Such questions were common to other colonial confessionals, including Motolonía (Fray Alonso de Molina)'s *Confesionario mayor* (1569).

32. O'Brien, "Many Meanings of *Aborto*," 954. Medina here might have been referring to a molar pregnancy, a complication of pregnancy in which an enlarged placenta but no fetus forms in the uterus, or in which only a nonviable fetus forms.

33. AGNM, Inquisición, vol. 561, exp. 6, fol. 557v. For an English translation of portions of Hernández's trial, see Jaffary and Mangan, "Isabel Hernández," 128–44.

34. AGNM, Inquisición, vol. 788, exp. 24, fols. 405v–406. I discussed de la Encarnación's appearances before the Inquisition in *False Mystics*, 47–49, 130. Christopoulos, *Abortion in Early Modern Italy*, 72, notes that the act of bleeding the foot to terminate a pregnancy described here may have been rooted in the European belief that the saphena vein was connected to the uterus. Bloodletting from this vein was believed to encourage contractions and menstruation and was frequently used to treat menstrual retention or induce abortion.

35. AGNM, Inquisición, vol. 788, exp. 24, fol. 503v.

36. AGNM, Inquisición, vol. 757, exp. 5, fol. 81; vol. 1328, fol. 400. I discussed Jesús María's case in *Reproduction and Its Discontents in Mexico*, 92, 94.

37. I located references to abortion in an additional four eighteenth-century Inquisition trials. No doubt others exist. But in none of the cases I have read did abortion feature prominently in the court's summation of the crimes for which defendants were accused or sentenced.

38. "La religión y la moral," *La voz de la religión*, May 23, 1949, 641. *Patria potestad* refers to the legal rights father had to control their children's financial and personal decisions until they reached the age of majority.

39. "Zacatecas," *El Siglo Diez y Nueve*, April 29, 1852, 3.

40. Luis G. de la Sierra, "El duelo y la autoridad pública," *El Foro*, August 27, 1874, 1.

41. Uribe-Uran, *Fatal Love*, 35–37, provides an excellent account of the Iberian sources judges relied upon in Spanish America.

42. There is a large literature on the Mexican Independence War; key recent works include Tutino, *Mexico City, 1808*; Rodríguez O., *"We Are Now the True Spaniards"*; and McEnroe, *From Colony to Nationhood in Mexico*.

43. Scardaville, "(Hapsburg) Law and (Bourbon) Order," 501–25; Owensby, *Empire of Law and Justice*; Premo, *Enlightenment on Trial*.

44. In 1835 Veracruz was one of the first states in Mexico to publish a criminal code preceding the Distrito Federal's 1871 code. The state of Mexico also published a penal code preceding the 1871 code, as did Oaxaca, which issued its first penal code one year before the capital. Beer, "Making Abortion Laws in Mexico," 49, notes that Veracruz's code decreed that a woman convicted for terminating a pregnancy should perform harsh labor for the rest of her life.

45. Roa Bárcena, *Manual razonado de práctica criminal*, 6.

46. Escriche y Martín, *Diccionario razonado*. Justices explicitly cited Escriche's text in many nineteenth-century infanticide and abortion trials, including AGEY, Justicia, Penal, caja 132, vol. 132, exp. 16; and caja 127, vol. 127, exp. 46, fol. 2v.

47. AGEY, Justicia, vol. 70, exp. 34, fol. 11. The statute is published in Dublán and Lozano, *Legislación Mexicana*, 817.

48. Archivo Histórico Judicial de Puebla (hereafter AHJP), exp. 10659.1, fol. 24.

49. AGEY, Justicia, Penal, vol. 70, exp. 34, fol. 1v. I have published an introduction to Sulú's trial along with photographs of excerpts of the original, transcriptions, and English translations on the History of Science in Latin America and the Caribbean (HOLSAC) website: https://mypages.unh.edu/hoslac/book/sulu-abortion.

50. AGEY, Justicia, Penal, vol. 70, exp. 34, fol. 2.

51. Real Academia Española, *Fuero juzgo*, 106. Here I quote from laws 2 and 3, of title 3, book 4, which I believe to be the relevant sections of the *Fuero juzgo*. Title 4 treats homicide more generally.

52. Real Academia Española, *Fuero juzgo*, 106.

53. AGEY, Justicia, Penal, vol. 70, exp. 34, fols. 2 and 26v.

54. López, *Las Siete Partidas* (1587), 7:30–30v.

55. López, *Las Siete Partidas* (1587), 7:31v. This punishment, as Bauman, *Crime and Punishment*, 23, notes, was derived from Roman law, where it was called the *poena cuellei*.

56. For example, the following cases refer to crimes of infanticide from the nineteenth-century Yucatán in which judges cited these articles of the *Partidas*: AGEY, Justicia, Penal, caja 101, vol. 101, exp. 6; caja 127, vol. 127, exp. 46.

57. Nieto de Piña, *Instruccion medica*, 24.

58. Cited in Dueñas Vargas, "Infanticidio y aborto en la colonia," 45. The reference here is to Archivo General de la Nación, Colombia, Colonial, Juicios Criminales, T. 86, fol. 697.

59. Escriche, *Diccionario razonado*, 27.

60. Escriche, *Diccionario razonado*, 27.

61. Escriche, *Diccionario razonado*, 28.

62. Escriche, *Diccionario razonado*, 28.

63. Lipsett Rivera, *Gender and the Negotiation of Daily Life*, 14.

64. García Goyena and Aguirre, *Febrero*, 228; Lucero, *Race and Reproduction in Cuba*, 326n59, describes it as a verse well known across Latin America and says it was a Spanish translation of an eighteenth-century French sonnet.

65. López, *Las Siete Partidas* (1555), 3:71.

66. The public defenders of Florencia May, Marcelina Ciua, and Severiana Cahum all make this argument for the absolution of their clients. AGEY, Justicia, Penal, caja 166, vol. 166, exp. 7; vol. 18, exp. 6, fol. 22; vol. 24, exp. 1. The judge in María Ines Pech's 1893 superior court affirmation of acquittal cited this section of the *Partidas* in his judgment. AGEY, Justicia, Penal, vol. 31, exp. 9.

67. AHJP, exp. 12745, fol. 68.

68. Justices referred to this passage, for example, in the following Yucatán reproductive crime cases: AGEY, Justicia, Penal, caja 101, vol. 101, exp. 6; caja 104, vol. 104, exp. 77; caja 117, vol. 117, exp. 20; caja 134, vol. 123, exp. 6; caja 135, vol. 135, exp. 10; caja 151, vol. 151, exp. 40.

69. López, *Las Siete Partidas* (1587), 7:94.

70. López, *Las Siete Partidas* (1587), 7:94.

71. AGEY, Justicia, Penal, vol. 70, exp. 34, fols. 27–27v.

72. The archives consulted were the Archivo General de la Nación, Mexico, Tribunal Superior de Justicia del Distrito Federal; the Archivo del Suprema Corte de Justicia de la Nación; the Archivo General del Estado de Yucatán; the Archivo Histórico Judicial de Puebla; the Archivo Histórico Judicial de Oaxaca; the Archivo Histórico del Estado de Tlaxcala; and the municipal archives of both Mexico City and Oaxaca City. I excluded from my examination those cases that, while they might have been labeled *abortos* in archival catalogs, are best understood as accidental miscarriages that were generally the result of violent acts committed against pregnant women and that unintentionally provoked miscarriages. Elizabeth Rodríguez Raygoza located an additional eleven abortion trials in Jalisco that opened between 1865 and 1873. See her "¿Víctimas o victimarias?"

73. AGNM, Indiferente Virreinal, caja 6473, exp. 29.

74. AGNM, Bienes Nacionales, vol. 731, exp. 4, fol. 8.

75. AGNM, Indiferente Virreinal, caja 5969, exp. 19.

76. Christopoulos, *Abortion in Early Modern Italy*; Spivack, "To Bring Down the Flowers," 107–51; Dayton, "Taking the Trade," 19–49.

77. Dore, "One Step Forward," 3–32.

78. Jaffary, *Reproduction and Its Discontents in Mexico*, 83.

79. Arrom, *Women of Mexico City*, 125. Historians have also unearthed instances earlier in the colonial period in other urban contexts, including seventeenth-century Guadalajara, of surprisingly low birth rates. Calvo, "Warmth of the Hearth," 291.

80. AGNM, Indiferente Virreinal, caja 5969, exp. 19.

81. Cohain, Buxbaum, and Mankuta, "Spontaneous First-Trimester Miscarriage Rates," 2.

82. Tanck de Estrada, "Muerte Precoz," 216.

83. This occurred in Milpa Alta in 1861. AGNM, TSJDF, caja 357; AHJO, Huajuapan, Criminal, leg. 33, exp. 5.

84. AHJP, Penal, caja 434, exp. 127, fols. 10v, 11, 14.

85. AHJP, Penal, caja 434, exp. 127, fols. 13v, 18v, 19.

86. AGEY, Justicia, Penal, vol. 70, exp. 34.

87. AGEY, Justicia, Penal, caja 69, vol. 69, exp. 83; caja 74, vol. 74, exp. 33; caja 106, vol. 106, exp. 85.

88. AGEY, Justicia, Penal, caja 122, vol. 122, exp. 32, fol. 1v.

89. Archivo Histórico Municipal de la Ciudad de Oaxaca, Serie: Juzgado de 1a Instancia, 1841–42, caja 27.

90. AHJO, Huajuapan, Criminal, leg. 3, exp. 7 (1826); leg. 33, exp. 5. In the first case, the judge did not pursue any investigation beyond a community member's denunciation that a woman who was impeding his son from marrying someone else had killed her fetus or newborn; in the second case, the defendant charged she had miscarried after the man who had impregnated her beat her. The court released the man from suspicion after eyewitnesses denied the incident, and although she was put *en depósito*, there is no record of a further criminal investigation.

91. The catalog does list one case indexed as an *aborto*. However, the instance involved an accidental abortion or what we might term a miscarriage.

92. The homicide figures are taken from the AGEY's electronic catalog.

93. Wellcome History of Medicine Library, Ferrer Espejo, "Lecciones de obstetricia," fol. 16c.

94. Schiebinger, *Plants and Empire*, 105–49.

95. Sahagún, *Historia general*, 2:605.

96. Sahagún, *Historia general*, 2:609.

97. Sahagún, *Historia general*, 2:609.

98. Hernández, *Qvatro libros de la naturaleza*, 6.

99. Hernández, *Qvatro libros de la naturaleza*, 5v, 15v.

100. Hernández, *Qvatro libros de la naturaleza*, 9, 92.

101. Quezada, "Creencias tradicionales," 232.

102. Emmart, *Badianus Manuscript*, 316.

103. Few, "Medical *Mestizaje*," 134; Quezada, "Métodos anticonceptivos," 232.

104. Holler, "Mixing/Medicines," 7.

105. Venegas, *Compendio de la medicina*, 242.

106. Huntington Library, León y Gama, "Medicina Mexicana," fols. 56, 70.

107. Núñez Cetina, "Reforma social," 102n86.

108. Huacuja, *Tratado práctico de partos*, 129.

109. Rodríguez, *Guía clínica*, 41.

110. Altamirano, "Algunos datos," 477.

111. Wellcome History of Medicine Library, "Noticia de varias plantas," fols. 4–4v. I am grateful to Farren Yero for sharing this source with me. Ralph Roys explains in his 1931 guide that Ibiña is a plant consisting of "a rosette of obovate leaves 3 to 10 cm long with a mass of fibrous roots, and floats on the surface of quiet water." Roys, *Ethnobotany of the Maya*, 247.

112. Wellcome History of Medicine Library, "Noticia de varias plantas," fol. 4v.

113. Riddle, *Contraception and Abortion*, 27.

114. Riddle, *Contraception and Abortion*, 20, 125.

115. Koblitz, *Sex and Herbs and Birth Control*, 10–11; Christopoulos, *Abortion in Early Modern Italy*, 75.

116. "Mixtura antimonial," *Suplemento a la Gazeta de México*, September 18, 1795, 419, 422.

117. Wellcome History of Medicine Library, "Magisterio rosada," fol. 26.

118. AHJP, Penal, exp. 12745, fols. 18–18v. Torres herself testified that she had taken only epazote to regularize her menses, fol. 13.

119. AHJP, Penal, caja 942, exp. 33204, fols. 14, 16v.

120. AGEY, Justicia, Penal, caja 130, vol. 130, exp. 10, fol. 3; Briggs, Freeman, and Yaffe, *Drugs in Pregnancy and Lactation*, 271.

121. Wellcome History of Medicine Library, "Prontuario o método fácil," fols. 14, 15–16. Another remedy described in the same work, the "Tintura para Epilepsia," was "prohibited from being given to women who were pregnant" (fol. 41).

122. AHJP, Penal, exp. 18168, fol. 30.

123. "Tribunales," *El Siglo Diez y Nueve*, November 11, 1852, 1.

124. AHJP, Penal, caja 1041, exp. 39046, fol. 25.

125. AHJP, Penal, caja 1041, exp. 39046, fol. 28.

126. AHJP, Penal, caja 1041, exp. 39046, fol. 28v.

127. Cházaro, "Mexican Women's Pelves," 100–115.

128. AHJP, Criminal, caja 634, exp. 19484, fol. 8v.

129. AHJP, Criminal, caja 1069, exp. 40734, fol. 1v.

130. AHJP, Penal, exp. 12745, fol. 54v.

131. For rich discussions of late eighteenth-century preoccupations with fetal and neonatal baptism, including through caesarean section, see Few, Tortorici, and Warren, *Baptism through Incision*; and O'Brien, *Surgery and Salvation*.

132. See, for example, Mauriceau, *Traité des maladies*, 292.

133. As encouraged, for example, in Segura, *Avisos saludables a las parteras*.

134. *Gazeta de México*, May 19, 1795, 250.

135. Ávila Espinosa, "Los niños abandonados," 49.

136. AGEY, Justicia, Penal, caja 95, vol. 95, exp. 9, fol. 5v.

137. AHJP, Penal, caja 634, exp. 19484, fol. 10.

138. AHJP, Penal, exp. 22524, fols. 3v–4.

139. Lipsett Rivera, *Origins of Macho*, 46.

140. Gonzalbo Aizpuru, "Familia y convivencia," 163–78.

141. Boyer, "Honor among Plebians," 152–78.

142. Shelton, *For Tranquility and Order*, 10.

143. Jaffary, *Reproduction and Its Discontents in Mexico*, 130–37.

144. AGEY, Justicia, Penal, vol. 60, exp. 33, fol. 7.

145. AHJO, Teposcolula, Penal, 1845, leg. 64, exp. 3.

146. AGEY, Justicia, Penal, caja 128, vol. 128, exp. 70, fols. 3v–4.

147. AGNM, Bandos, vol. 24, exp. 55, fol. 143.

2. 1871–1930

1. Breña, "Juicio crítico," 257.

2. The distinction is explained by Cruz, *¿Existen indicaciones?*, 9. The 1871 penal code of the Distrito Federal termed *parto prematuro artificial* the interruption of pregnancy beginning in the eighth month of pregnancy. López Hermosa, "Medicina legal," 193.

3. Breña, "Juicio crítico," 261 (emphasis in the original).

4. Breña, "Juicio crítico," 275.

5. "Programas para la Escuela Nacional de Medicina," 503.

6. Urías Horcasitas, "Eugenesia y aborto en México," 310–11.

7. Standard works on the revolution—its causes and its development—are Womack, *Zapata and the Mexican Revolution*; Knight, *Mexican Revolution*; and Becker, *Setting the Virgin on Fire*.

8. The Partido Revolucionario Institucional was founded in 1929 and was first called the Partido Nacional Revolucionario, then rechristened the Partido Nacional Revolucionario, and renamed the PRI in 1946.

9. O'Brien, "Tacit Pact with the State," 60.

10. Olcott, Vaughan, and Cano, *Sex in Revolution*.

11. Martínez de Castro, *Exposición de motivos del código penal*, 2.

12. Martínez de Castro, *Exposición de motivos del código penal*, 2–3.

13. Núñez, "Imaginario médico y práctica jurídica," 142.

14. *Código penal para el Distrito Federal* (1871), cap. 9, art. 569, 146–47.

15. *Código penal para el Distrito Federal* (1871), cap. 9, art. 572, 147.

16. *Código penal para el Distrito Federal* (1871), cap. 9, art. 573, 147.

17. Article 16, though, indicated that the determination of whether a crime was *leve* (light) or *grave* rested with the "prudent assessment of the judges," who should consider the intent to eliminate harm, as well as the social position of defendants (sex, age, education, instruction, and social position). *Código penal para el Distrito Federal* (1871), cap. 1, art. 16, 7.

18. Martínez de Castro, *Exposición de motivos del código penal*, 45.

19. *Código penal para el Distrito Federal* (1871), cap. 9, art. 584, 149.

20. Here Mexico's position was in line with liberal codes adopted elsewhere in Latin America. In Colombia, for example, between 1837 and 1936, therapeutic abortion was lawful in cases where pregnancy or birth endangered the life of the pregnant woman. A great deal of Argentine scholarship argued that the privileging of the discourse of female sexual honor operated as an attenuating influence in reproductive crimes in the late nineteenth century. Peru's first penal code, framed in in 1836, was considerably harsher and classified abortion as homicide.

21. López Sánchez, "La centralidad del útero y sus anexos," 165.

22. Hidalgo y Carpio and Ruiz y Sandoval, *Compendio de medicina legal*, 163.

23. Martínez de Castro, *Exposición de motivos del código penal*, 45.

24. Núñez, "Imaginario médico y práctica jurídica," 10; Rivera Reynaldos, "Crímenes pasionales," par. 2.

25. Núñez, "Imaginario médico y práctica jurídica," 21.

26. Núñez Cetina, "Reforma social," 72–73, 107.

27. Núñez Cetina, "Reforma social," 72.

28. Rivera Reynaldos, "Crímenes pasionales," par. 4.

29. *Código criminal y penal del estado libre y soberano de Oaxaca*, tít. 2, arts. 847–55, 208–9.

30. *Código penal para el Distrito Federal* (1876), tit. II, cap. 9, 141–44. Various other states adopted the 1871 Distrito Federal code the same year.

31. *Código penal del estado de Yucatán*, cap. 9, arts. 474–85, 96–97.

32. *Código penal del estado libre y soberna de Tlaxcala*, cap. 9, arts. 456, 458, 117. The state of Veracruz, unusually, produced a penal code in 1835, based largely on the Spanish penal code of 1822, that sentenced those convicted of abortion to harsh labor for the rest of their lives. Both Hidalgo and Durango also began developing codes before the Federal District and briefly addressed abortion in these, calling for slightly longer terms of imprisonment than did the capital's code. Both states subsequently adopted most of the 1871 provisions.

33. The judicial archives of Yucatán are housed within the state archives (Archivo General del Estado de Yucatán), as is the case for Tlaxcala (Archivo Histórico del Estado de

Tlaxcala). In Oaxaca the judicial archives are housed in an independent archive, the Archivo Histórico Judicial de Oaxaca (AHJO), although, when I used these archives, the state archives staff told me there are plans to incorporate the collection into the general state archive, the Archivo General del Estado de Oaxaca. These repositories all have the advantage of housing materials spanning from the viceregal period through the early twentieth century, making the collections particularly useful in terms of examining change over time. In the AHJO I searched the holdings of four districts from the colonial period up to 1900: Villa Alta, Teposcolula, Hujuapan, and Ejutla. I have also included material I found in the Archivo Histórico Municipal de la Ciudad de Oaxaca, one case located in the Archivo del Suprema Corte de Justicia in Mexico City, and one from the Tribunal Superior de Justicia del Distrito Federal housed in the Archivo General de la Nación, México.

34. AGEY, Justicia, Penal, caja 128, vol. 128, exp. 70, fols. 3–4. *Estupro* is often translated as "rape," or the rape of a virgin. But in *Heart in a Glass Jar*, 23, William E. French points out it is more accurate to understand the term as referring to copulation with a chaste woman.

35. Zahler, "Reforming Women, Protecting Men," 485. Zahler credits David Carey with the term.

36. Speckman Guerra, *Crimen y castigo*, 65. Here again, however, some of these cases likely referred to unintentional miscarriages rather than procured abortions.

37. Zero cases in Tlaxcala, three cases in Oaxaca, and five in Yucatán in the whole period prior to 1871.

38. "Sucesos de Policía," *El Republicano*, May 31, 1879, 2.

39. "Aborto," *La Libertad*, August 6, 1878, 2. Many other such reports can be found in newspapers from the 1870s–1910s, including "Un feto abandon: Madre infame," *El Popular*, November 8, 1899, 1; and "Madre Criminal," *El Continente Americano*, November 8, 1899, 2.

40. "Infame," *La Orquesta*, June 3, 1871, 1.

41. The AHJO houses the records of ten judicial districts, from 1560 to 1949. I have consulted the records for four of these—Villa Alta, Teposcolula, Ejutla, and Huajuapan—from the earliest periods up until 1900.

42. Hidalgo y Carpio and Ruiz y Sandoval, *Compendio de medicina legal*, 173.

43. Núñez, "Imaginario médico y práctica jurídica," 129.

44. Núñez, "Imaginario médico y práctica jurídica," 129n3.

45. McCaa, "Peopling of Nineteenth-Century Mexico," 620.

46. Núñez Cetina found that some of the women in the six abortion cases she located between 1920 and 1940 came from the middle class. "Reforma social," 89.

47. *Periódico Oficial del Estado de Chihuahua*, October 17, 1925, 6.

48. AGEY, Justicia, vol. 69, exp. 48.

49. AGEY, Justicia, vol. 69, exp. 48.

50. AGEY, Judicial, Penal, vol. 132, exp. 34, fol. 8v.

51. Archivo Histórico del Estado de Tlaxcala (AHET), Justicia, Criminal, caja 376, exp. 17, fol. 1v.

52. "Repugnantes crímenes: una casera cómplice. La autoridad debe intervenir," *El Demócrata,* April 6, 1895, 2.

53. "Consignación de dos Magistrados," *El Tiempo,* June 19, 1907, 2.

54. Núñez Cetina, "Reforma social," 89.

55. Hidalgo y Carpio and Ruiz y Sandoval, *Compendio de medicina legal,* 177–82.

56. Fernando Altamirano, "Leguminosas indígena medicinales," *La Naturaleza,* January 1, 1877, 104.

57. Duque de Estrada, "La embriotomía"; *Crónica médica Mexicana,* August 1, 1897, 33.

58. Duque de Estrada, "La embriotomía," 33.

59. "Secretaría de Estado y del despacho de gobernación," *El Siglo Diez y Nueve,* September 7, 1880, 2.

60. Archivo Histórico de la Secretaría de Salud, Beneficencia Pública, Establecimiento Hospitalarios, Hospital de Maternidad y de Infancia, leg. 6, exp. 16.

61. Archivo Histórico de la Secretaría de Salud, Beneficencia Pública, leg. 2, exp. 29. Another condemnation of a midwife's criminal administration of cihuapatli to induce an abortion appears in "Contra María Concepcion Mejia por infanticidio," AGNM, TSJDF, 1880, caja 681, fol. 8.

62. AGEY, Justicia, Penal, caja 533, vol. 29, exp. 40, fols. 7v, 9.

63. AGEY, Justicia, Penal, caja 533, vol. 29, exp. 40, fols. 10–10v.

64. Jaffary, *Reproduction and Its Discontents in Mexico,* 81–82. Cosminsky, *Midwives and Mothers,* 117, finds that Mayan midwives in Guatemala continue to use artemisia (another name for *altamisa*) as both an emmenagogue and an abortifacient up to the present.

65. I have indicated cases as "acquitted" in table 1 when justices issued such a judgment or when the absence of sentencing indicates the case did not proceed to that resolution.

66. Archivo Histórico del Estado de Tlaxcala (AHET), Justicia, Criminal, caja 376, exp. 17, fol. 1.

67. *Código penal del estado libre y soberna de Tlaxcala,* cap. 9, art. 459, 117.

68. AGNM, TSJDF, 1883, caja 841, fols. 18, 22.

69. Menocal, *Estudio sobre el aborto en México,* 5–20.

70. Speckman Guerra, "Morir a manos de una mujer," 293; Núñez Cetina, "Reforma social," 82, 107; Jaffary, *Reproduction and Its Discontents in Mexico,* 129; Shelton, "Infanticidio y disciplina popular," 291.

71. AJHO, Teposcolula, Penal, leg. 105, exp. 29, fol. 5.

72. AGEY, Justicia, Penal, vol. 60, exp. 33, fol. 7.

73. AHJO, Villa Alta, Criminal, leg. 109, exp. 3.

74. AHJO, Villa Alta, Criminal, leg. 109, exp. 3.

75. AHJO, Villa Alta, Criminal, leg. 109, exp. 3.

76. AHJO, Teposcolula, Criminal, leg. 107, exp. 27, fol. 1.

77. AHJO, Teposcolula, Criminal, leg. 107, exp. 27, fol. 1. In this instance "free" referred to the fact that Ana Vázquez was not legally under the tutelage of a man—a husband, father, or uncle.

78. AHJO, Teposcolula, Criminal, leg. 107, exp. 27, fol. 2v.

79. AHJO, Villa Alta, Criminal, leg. 108, exp. 3.

80. AHJO, Villa Alta, Penal, leg. 127, exp. 30.

81. AGEY, Justicia, Penal, caja 529, vol. 25, exp. 20, fol. 1.

82. AGNM, TSJDF, 1883, caja 841, fol. 2.

83. AHJO, Villa Alta, Criminal, caja 125, exp. 6, fol. 2.

84. AHJO, Villa Alta, Criminal, caja 125, exp. 6, fol. 19.

85. "Inmoralidad y crimen," *La Patria*, September 7, 1897, 3.

86. Federici, *Caliban and the Witch*, 36, 88. Federici locates the peak of such surveillance in the European context in the era of demographic collapse due to the black plague in the late fourteenth century and in the early modern expansion of mercantilism.

87. Rivera Reynaldos, "Crímenes pasionales," par. 2; Overmyer-Velázquez, *Visions of the Emerald City*.

88. Speckman Guerra, "Disorder and Control," 74.

89. Porter, *From Angel to Office Worker*, 10–11.

90. Toxqui, "Breadwinners or Entrepreneurs," 109, notes that while one-third of the labor force was female in 1811, with over half working as domestic servants or in food-related industries, by 1895 almost half of the labor force was female, and over 20 percent worked in processing industries. See also Porter, *From Angel to Office Worker*, 4–5, on the intensification of women's work outside the home beginning in the late nineteenth century.

91. Shelton, "Infanticidio y disciplina popular," 259.

92. Shelton, "Birth and Death in the Maternity Ward," 40.

93. Hidalgo y Carpio, "Jurisprudencia Médica," 300.

94. Blum, *Domestic Economies*, xvi.

95. Blum, *Domestic Economies*, 85.

96. Núñez Cetina, "Reforma social," 72, 80.

97. Núñez Cetina, "Reforma social," 72.

98. O'Brien, *Surgery and Salvation*, chapters 1 and 2.

99. *Diccionario de ciencias eclesiásticas*, 71. Núñez indicates that this text was consulted and circulated in Mexico. "Imaginario médico y práctica jurídica," 139.

100. *Diccionario de ciencias eclesiásticas*, 69.

101. *Diccionario de ciencias eclesiásticas*, 72. Núñez's discussion of it directed my reading of the *Diccionario*.

102. Ortiz-Ortega, "Law and the Politics of Abortion," 197.

103. Ortiz-Ortega, "Feminist Demand for Legal Abortion," 85.

104. Ortiz-Ortega, "Feminist Demand for Legal Abortion," 86.

105. Monlau, *El libro de los casados*, 2:426.

106. Monlau, *El libro de los casados*, 2:426.

107. O'Brien, "Many Meanings of *Aborto*," 957.

108. Breña, "Juicio crítico," 266.

109. AGEY, Justicia, Penal, caja 517, exp. 4, fol. 3v.

110. O'Brien, *Salvation and Surgery*, 117–29.

111. Navarro y Cardona, *Del parto prematuro en México*, 15–16.

112. Navarro y Cardona, *Del parto prematuro en México*, 18.

113. Navarro y Cardona, *Del parto prematuro en México*, 40.

114. Navarro y Cardona, *Del parto prematuro en México*, 41.

115. O'Brien, "Many Meanings of *Aborto*."

116. Along with the works discussed here, many other theses and tracts published between 1871 and 1930 discussed surgical abortions. They include Ibáñez, *Someras reflexiones*; Gómez, *Tratamiento del aborto*; Ibarra, *Tratamiento de las complicaciones del aborto*; Alvear, *Ligeros apuntes sobre etiología y profilaxia del aborto*; Villalobos Quijano, *Aborto médico*; López Hermosa, *Aborto en sus relaciones con la legislación penal*; Mayer, *El aspecto médico-legal del aborto*; Torre, *Ensayo de estudios sobre uno de los problemas médico-legales*; and Trens Marentes, *Estudio de las complicaciones del aborto*.

117. O'Brien, "Tacit Pact with the State," 116.

118. "Los médicos criminales," *El Popular*, October 27, 1898, 1. Abrego's story is treated in Garza, *Imagined Underworld*.

119. Troconis y Alcalá, *En los embarazos tiernos*.

120. Tajonar y Cardosa, *Breve estudio comparativo*.

121. Escriche y Martín, *Diccionario razonado*, 1:36.

122. "El Poder Teocratico," *El monitor republicano*, October 10, 1855, 1.

123. Both Cruz and López Hermosa, "Medicina legal," declared that this was the position a majority of contemporaneous physicians, including Carona y Valle, Lavista, Licéaga, Gutiérrez, Zárraga, and Mejía, supported.

124. Cruz, *¿Existen indicaciones?*, 10.

125. Hidalgo y Carpio and Ruiz y Sandoval, *Compendio de medicina legal*, 1:182–84.

126. Hidalgo y Carpio and Ruiz y Sandoval, *Compendio de medicina legal*, 1:184.

127. Hidalgo y Carpio and Ruiz y Sandoval, *Compendio de medicina legal*, 1:179, 180.

128. Duque de Estrada, "Aborto Provocado," 173–75.

129. This condition translates literally to "pregnancy self-poisoning." I am unsure from the context as to whether he meant to refer to edema or intensive, chronic vomiting.

130. Duque de Estrada, "Aborto Provocado," 175.

131. Duque de Estrada, "La embriotomía," 36.

132. "Exámen científico," *La voz de México*, December 16, 1877, 3.

133. "Reglamento y arancel del Consejo Médico-Legal," 225.

134. Shelton, "Birth and Death in the Maternity Ward," 39.

135. *El Heraldo Médico*, March 15, 1908, 19.

136. *El Pueblo*, September 24, 1916, 7.

137. O'Brien, *Surgery and Salvation*, 111.

3. 1931–2000

1. "La Asamblea de cirujanos," *El Informador*, November 12, 1952, 1.

2. Marta Lamas, one of the founders of GIRE, has long been an important activist and researcher on abortion in Mexico. Among her important works is *La interrupción legal del embarazo*. I have also drawn heavily from Adriana Ortiz-Ortega's extensive publications, dating back to her doctoral dissertation, "The Feminist Demand for Legal Abortion." Research by Martha Santillán Esqueda, Saydi Núñez Cetina, Elizabeth O'Brien, Caroline Beer, and many author scholars cited below has all been tremendously helpful.

3. See Nelson, "Feminism, Human Rights, and Abortion Debates," 119–40, for a discussion of how the discourse of human rights animated both pro- and anti-abortion campaigns at the time of these proposed legal changes.

4. Buffington, "Looking Forward," 24.

5. Secretaria de Gobernación, *Código penal* (1929), cap. 8, arts. 831–39, 188–89.

6. Secretaria de Gobernación, *Código penal* (1929), cap. 9, art. 1000, 219.

7. Secretaria de Gobernación, *Código penal* (1929), cap. 9, art. 1001, 220.

8. Buffington, "Looking Forward," 28.

9. Secretaria de Gobernación, *Código penal* (1931), art. 333, 70; Barreda Solórzano, *El delito de aborto*, 43–44.

10. Secretaria de Gobernación, *Código penal* (1931), art. 329, 70.

11. Secretaria de Gobernación, *Código penal* (1931), art. 334, 71.

12. González Mariscal, "Evolución del aborto en México," 1326.

13. Barraza, *Aborto y pena en México*, 85.

14. Elvia Carrillo Puerto had founded Mexico's first feminist league in 1912 and was also the first woman elected as a state deputy in 1919.

15. Galindo, "La Mujer en el Porvenir."

16. Foppa and Aguilar, "First Feminist Congress in Mexico, 1916," 196.

17. Cabrera, "Demographic Dynamics and Development," 108.

18. Sanger, "La regulación de la natalidad."

19. Cano, "Una perspectiva del aborto," 363.

20. For further discussion of these programs, see Sanders, *Gender and Welfare in Mexico*.

21. For further discussion, see Sanders, *Gender and Welfare in Mexico*, 8–10.

22. Urías Horcasitas, "Eugenesia y aborto en México," 307–9. Urías's article led me to several of the contemporary sources to which I refer in this discussion.
23. Suárez y Lopez-Guazo, "Mexican Eugenics Society," 146.
24. Sanders, "Women, Sex, and the 1950s Acción Católica," 270–97.
25. Sánchez-Rivera, "Making of 'La Gran Familia Mexicana,'" 165.
26. Saavedra, "Aborto Criminal," 624, 627; Urías Horcasitas, "Eugenesia y aborto en México," 314.
27. Saavedra, "Aborto Criminal," 627.
28. Escontria, "La Eugenesia y la Limitación de Natalidad," 415.
29. Gastélum, "Tratamiento del aborto," 541.
30. Gastélum, "Tratamiento del aborto," 541.
31. In "Many Meanings of *Aborto*," 961, O'Brien describes another contemporary physician, Alfredo Islas Hernández, who supported therapeutic abortions including in cases of rape in the 1930s. Urías Horcasitas, "Eugenesia y aborto en México," 321, notes that Islas Hernández also advocated for abortion's validity in the cases of various illnesses including tuberculosis and insanity.
32. Gastélum, "Tratamiento del aborto," 542.
33. Stern, "'Hour of Eugenics' in Veracruz," 431–43.
34. "Código penal para el estado de Sonora," *Periódico Oficial del Estado de Sonora*, November 16, 1940, cap. 4, art. 204, 55. My research assistant in the Sonora state archives, Benjamin Alonso, could not locate any abortion trials that involved this clause.
35. Quoted in Barraza, *Aborto y pena en México*, 86.
36. Maier, "Documenting Mexico's Culture War," 158.
37. Cabrera, "Demographic Dynamics and Development," 108. Schell, "Gender, Class, and Anxiety," 121, discusses the scandalous rumor that a Mexico City vocational school was distributing Sanger's pamphlet to its students.
38. Boylan, "Revolutionary and Not-So-Revolutionary Negotiations," 167.
39. Urías Horcasitas, "Eugenesia y aborto en México," 310n10.
40. Ornelas Méndez, *Inventario*, 33.
41. O'Brien, "Tacit Pact with the State," 60.
42. Narvaez, "Interrupción terapéutica," 89.
43. Narvaez, "Interrupción terapéutica," 91. The term *laminaria* referred to a genus of seaweed that could be sterilized and used for cervical dilation. Oxytocins are naturally or chemically produced hormones that stimulate contractions.
44. Narvaez, "Interrupción terapéutica," 92.
45. O'Brien, "Many Meanings of *Aborto*," 962.
46. Perera Castillo, "Lugar de la cirugía en el aborto," 385. I have been unable to find a translation of the term *riletrorragias*, although its suffix indicates it involves a form of hemorrhage.

47. Perera Castillo, "Lugar de la cirugía en el aborto," 397.

48. Smithe, "Breve estudio"; Marin, "Sobre la legislación del aborto," 106, referred to one such article, "Algunas consideraciones sobre la legislación del aborto," published in the October 1946 edition of the medical journal *Sugestiones*.

49. Santillán Esqueda, *Delincuencia femenina*, 156.

50. González Mariscal, "Evolución del aborto en México," 1325; Ortiz-Ortega, "Feminist Demand for Legal Abortion," 120.

51. Núñez Cetina, "Reforma social," 90; Santillán Esqueda, "Maternidad y transgresiones," 1126n25.

52. "Estadísticas," *El Informador*, April 21, 1936, 5.

53. "Comentarios," *Gaceta médica de México*, January 1932, 21.

54. "Correspondencia del puerto de Mazatlán," *El Informador*, July 19, 1939, 8.

55. "Ingresaron a la penitencia," *El Informador*, June 12, 1954, 16.

56. "Encuesta sobre el Aborto en México," *Sucesos Para Todos*, October 30, 1971, 28, 29.

57. Barreda Solórzano, *El delito de aborto*, 24.

58. Cantú et al., "Actitud del médico ante el aborto," 281.

59. Barreda Solórzano, *El delito de aborto*, 24.

60. Ortiz-Ortega, "Entrevista a Luis de la Barreda," 32.

61. Erviti, *El aborto entre mujeres pobres*, 105.

62. Viesca Benavides, de Lara, and Valdes Muriel, "Consideraciones Sociales," 182.

63. Viesca Benavides, de Lara, and Valdes Muriel, "Consideraciones Sociales," 183.

64. Viesca Benavides, de Lara, and Valdes Muriel, "Consideraciones Sociales," 192 (emphasis in the original).

65. Martinez, "Contribución al Estudio," 258.

66. Martinez, "Contribución al Estudio," 258.

67. Martinez, "Contribución al Estudio," 259.

68. Martinez, "Contribución al Estudio," 260.

69. "Piden los Cirujanos más Castigo Para el Aborto," *El Porvenir*, November 20, 1958, 2.

70. Gastélum, "¿Es el aborto provocado un recurso terapéutico?," 453.

71. Gastélum, "¿Es el aborto provocado un recurso terapéutico?," 453.

72. Marván, "¿Es el aborto provocado un recurso terapéutico," 459–61.

73. Academia Nacional de Medicina, "Actas de la Academia Nacional de Medicina," 839.

74. Pérez Molina, Díaz Estua, and Bazán, "Consideraciones sobre el aborto terapéutico," 251.

75. Pérez Molina, Díaz Estua, and Bazán, "Consideraciones sobre el aborto terapéutico," 255.

76. Nigenda and Solórzano, "Doctors and Corporatist Politics," 73–99.

77. Loeza, "La iglesia y la educación en México," 185.

78. "Merece Condena en Todo Caso el Aborto Criminal," *El Informador*, January 15, 1969, 8.

79. Gonzáles Santos, *Portrait of Assisted Reproduction in Mexico*, 70.

80. Cantú et al., "Actitud del médico ante el aborto," 281–83.

81. Two exceptions are Cantú et al., "Actitud del médico ante el aborto"; and Souza Machorro, "Aborto electivo," 119–22.

82. González M., "La penalización del aborto en México," 50.

83. González M., "La penalización del aborto en México," 50.

84. Gonzáles de León Aguirre and Salinas Urbina, "Los médicos en formación y el aborto," 227–36.

85. Lamas, *Interrupción legal del embarazo,* 56.

86. Erviti, Castro, and Sosa Sánchez, "Las luchas clasificatorias," 660.

87. Juárez et al., *Unintended Pregnancy and Induced Abortion,* 10, 11.

88. Barreda Solórzano, *El delito de aborto,* 29.

89. Juárez et al., *Unintended Pregnancy and Induced Abortion,* 21.

90. Juárez et al., *Unintended Pregnancy and Induced Abortion,* 22.

91. Ortiz-Ortega, "Feminist Demand for Legal Abortion," 21.

92. Tarrés, "El movimiento de mujeres y el sistema político mexicano," 366.

93. Lamas, "La despenalización del aborto en México," 157.

94. Beer, "Making Abortion Laws in Mexico," 50.

95. Cano, "Una perspectiva del aborto en los años treinta," 362.

96. Maier, "Documenting Mexico's Culture War," 158.

97. For a discussion of GIRE's historical development, see Lamas, "Feminist Movement," 58–67.

98. Cabrera, "Demographic Dynamics and Development," 109.

99. Cabrera, "Demographic Dynamics and Development," 109.

100. Espinosa Tavares, "They Are Coming in So Fast," 76–96; Opperman, "There Was No 'Family Planning Movement,'" 97–118.

101. Quoted in Márquez Murrieta, "Aborto y derechos reproductivos," 185.

102. For further discussion of this shift in state policy, see Singer, *Lawful Sins,* 46–48.

103. Márquez Murrieta, "Aborto y derechos reproductivos," 185.

104. Ortiz-Ortega, "Feminist Demand for Legal Abortion," 187.

105. Beer, "Making Abortion Laws in Mexico," 42.

106. Beer, "Making Abortion Laws in Mexico," 42.

107. Ortiz-Ortega, "Feminist Demand for Legal Abortion," 188; Beer, "Making Abortion Laws in Mexico," 41.

108. "Necesario Limitar a Tres los Hijos de Cada Pareja," *El Informador,* July 10, 1978, 13-A.

109. "El PDM, Contra el Proyecto de Legalización del Aborto," *El Informador,* November 22, 1979, 2-C.

110. Conrado Zuckermann, "El Aborto," *El Informador,* January 4, 1980, 2-A.

111. Beer, "Making Abortion Laws in Mexico," 41.

112. One of the additional curiosities of this pattern of uneven abortion liberalization across states is that it is not the case that some of the most conservative and religious states in the country (Puebla and Jalisco) adopted the most conservative abortion regulation.

113. These groupings come from Ortiz-Ortega, "Politics of Abortion in Mexico," 159–60. I modified her classification of Sonora in the most conservative group, having located the 1940 penal code whereby that state declared eugenic abortions lawful.

114. Beer, "Making Abortion Laws in Mexico," 51.

115. "Encuesta sobre el Aborto en México," *Sucesos Para Todos*, October 30, 1971, 30.

116. Chihuahua, however, removed nonpenalization for economic reasons from its state penal code in 1987. Guerrero and Hidalgo eventually added socioeconomic considerations to their codes. Barraza, *Aborto y pena en México*, 85.

117. Barreda Solórzano, *El delito de aborto*, 30.

118. Belausteguigoitia, "El aborto en México," 77.

119. Vela, "Current Abortion Regulation in Mexico," 12.

120. *Código penal para el Distrito Federal* (1871), tít. 6, cap. 2, art. 787, 199.

121. *Código penal para el Distrito Federal* (1871), tít. 2, cap. 1, art. 34, 12.

122. Núñez Cetina, "Reforma social," 75.

123. Jiménez Huerta, "Delito de infanticidio," 112.

124. Article 27 of the Ley Federal de Archivos (2012) protects the confidentiality of individuals whose records are held in state archives.

125. Jiménez Huerta, "Delito de infanticidio," 114.

126. Pavón Vasconcelos, "El delito de aborto," 604 (emphasis in the original).

127. Sen. Javier Orozco Gómez, "Iniciativas," *Gaceta del Senado*, December 14, 2011, https://www.senado.gob.mx/64/gaceta_del_senado/documento/33557.

128. Madrazo, "Evolution of Mexico City's Abortion Laws," 267.

129. Stevenson, "Gender Politics and Policy Process in Mexico," 282.

130. Stevenson, "Gender Politics and Policy Process in Mexico," 282.

131. Barraza, *Aborto y pena en México*, 94.

132. Pérez Duarte y N., "El aborto en nuestra república," 39.

133. Vela, "Current Abortion Regulation in Mexico," 13.

134. Ferreira, "Problemas legales," 13–15.

135. González-Santos, *Portrait of Assisted Reproduction in Mexico*, 130.

136. Cesar Cepada, "Reformas al Código provocarían libertinaje sexual," *El Norte*, November 27, 1995, 1.

137. Stein, "Embryo Research."

138. *Código penal para el Distrito Federal*, (2002) Libro Segundo, parte Especial, tít. 2, cap. 1, art. 149, accessed May 25, 2024.

139. The state of Puebla made a similar revision in 2012. Gobierno del Estado de Puebla, *Código penal del estado libre y soberano de Puebla*, 188.

140. "Enérgica Denuncia del Aborto," *El Informador*, January 2, 1977, 1.

141. Ortiz-Ortega, "Feminist Demand for Legal Abortion," 50–51.

142. "Preocupación de la Iglesia por la Mentalidad Abortista," *El Informador*, December 1, 1976, 1.

143. Barreda Solórzano, *El delito de aborto*, 71.

144. Cabrera, "Demographic Dynamics and Development," 112.

145. Lamas and Bisell, "Abortion and Politics in Mexico," 12.

146. Arguedas Ramírez and Morgan, "Reproductive Rights Counteroffensive in Mexico," 423, 424.

147. Jelen, Roth-Johnson, and Tuman, "Culture Wars in Latin America," 4, 5.

148. *Código penal del estado de Chihuahua*, art. 219; *Código penal del estado libre y soberano de Puebla*, art. 343.

149. Lamas, *La interrupción legal del embarazo*, 34.

150. Madrazo, "Narratives of Prenatal Personhood," 337.

151. Beer, "Making Abortion Laws in Mexico," 50.

152. Maier, "Documenting Mexico's Culture War," 157.

153. Stevenson, "Gender Politics and Policy Process," 277.

154. Stevenson, "Gender Politics and Policy Process," 278.

155. Wilson et al., "Public Opinion on Abortion," 178.

Conclusion

1. Monsiváis, "When Gender Can't Be Seen," 17; O'Brien, "Tacit Pact with the State," 57.

2. O'Brien, "Tacit Pact with the State," 18.

3. Sanders, "Women, Sex, and the 1950s Acción Católica," 270–97.

4. Sanders, "Gender and Welfare Reform," 170. See also her discussion of institutional promotion of motherhood in the 1940s and 1950s in *Gender and Welfare in Mexico*.

5. Santillán Esqueda, *Mujeres criminales*, 140.

6. Ana Salado, "El modernismo," *Excelsior*, April 27, 1941, 3; cited in Santillán, *Mujeres criminales*, 145.

7. Quoted in Alexander, *Sons of the Mexican Revolution*, 4.

8. Porter, *From Angel to Office Worker*, 206–7.

9. Porter, *From Angel to Office Worker*, 207.

10. Cantú et al., "Actitud del médico ante el aborto," 283.

11. Cook, Erdman, and Dickens, "Introduction," 3.

12. Siegel, "Constitutionalization of Abortion," 14.

13. Siegel, "Constitutionalization of Abortion," 34.

14. Williams, "Problem of Perspective," 9–14.

BIBLIOGRAPHY

Archives and Manuscript Materials

Archivo del Suprema Corte de Justicia de la Nación

Archivo General de la Nación, Colombia

    Colonial, Juicios Criminales

Archivo General de la Nación, Mexico (AGNM)

    Bienes Nacionales

    Indiferente Virreinal

    Inquisición

    Tribunal Superior de Justicia del Distrito Federal (TSJDF)

Archivo General del Estado de Yucatán (AGEY)

    Justicia

Archivo Histórico de la Secretaría de Salud

    Beneficencia Pública, Establecimiento Hospitalarios, Hospital de Maternidad y de Infancia

Archivo Histórico del Estado de Oaxaca

Archivo Histórico del Estado de Tlaxcala (AHET)

Archivo Histórico Judicial de Oaxaca (AHJO)

    Ejutla, Criminal

    Huajuapan, Criminal

    Teposcolula, Criminal

    Villa Alta, Criminal

Archivo Histórico Judicial de Puebla (AHJP)

Archivo Histórico Municipal de la Ciudad de Oaxaca

Huntington Library

    Antonio de León y Gama, "Medicina Mexicana," HM 4297

University of Arizona Library Special Collections, Tucson

"Casos reservados sinodales en la Diocesis de Mexico, y privilegios de los Indios en esta material" (ca. eighteenth century, MS 130)

Wellcome History of Medicine Library

José Ferrer Espejo, "Lecciones de obstetricia, dadas oralmente para curso de segundo año por su catedrático, J. Ferrer Espejo" (Mexico City, 1854, Ms. Amer. 122)

"Magisterio rosada" (Ms. Am. 58)

"Noticia de varias plantas [de Yucatán] y sus virtudes" (Ms. Am. 17)

"Prontuario o método fácil en donde se contienen las mas eficaces Medicinas" (Ms. Am. 18)

Published Works

Academia Nacional de Medicina. "Actas de la Academia Nacional de Medicina, 1958–1959." *Gaceta médica de México* 88, no. 11 (November 1958): 829–40.

Alexander, Ryan M. *Sons of the Mexican Revolution: Miguel Alemán and His Generation*. Albuquerque: University of New Mexico Press, 2016.

Altamirano, Fernando. "Algunos datos farmacológicos acerca de catorce Mexicanas." In *Transactions of the First Pan-American Medical Congress*, 474–79. Washington DC: Government Printing Office, 1895.

Alva, Bartolomé de. *A Guide to Confession Large and Small in the Mexican Language, 1634*. Edited by Barry D. Sell, John Frederick Schwaller, and Lu Ann Homza. Norman: University of Oklahoma Press, 1999.

Alvear, Manuel. *Ligeros apuntes sobre etiología y profilaxia del aborto*. Mexico City: Tipografía de F. P. Hoeck y Comp., 1900.

Arguedas Ramírez, Gabriela, and Lynn M. Morgan. "The Reproductive Rights Counteroffensive in Mexico and Central America." *Feminist Studies* 43, no. 2 (2017): 423–37.

Aristotle. *The Basic Works of Aristotle*. Edited by Richard KcKeon. New York: Random House, 1941.

———. *History of Animals*. Book 7. Translated by D'Arcy Wentworth Thompson. Accessed February 7, 2024. http://classics.mit.edu/Aristotle/history_anim.7.vii.html.

———. *On the Generation of Animals*. Book 2. Accessed February 7, 2024. http://www.esp.org/books/aristotle/generation-of-animals/html/index.p.3.html.

Arrom, Silvia Marina. *The Women of Mexico City, 1790–1857*. Stanford CA: Stanford University Press, 1985.

Ávila Espinosa, Felipe Arturo. "Los niños abandonados de la casa de niños expósitos de la ciudad de México: 1767–1821." In *La familia en el mundo iberoamericano*, edited by Pilar Gonzalbo Aizpuru and Cecilia Rabell, 265–310. Mexico City: Instituto de Investigaciones Sociales, Universidad Nacional Autónoma de México, 1994.

Barraza, Eduardo. *Aborto y pena en México*. Mexico City: Instituto Nacional de Ciencias Penales, 2003.

Barreda Solórzano, Luis de la. *El delito de aborto: una careta de buena conciencia*. Mexico City: Miguel Ángel Porrúa, 1991.

Bauman, Richard. *Crime and Punishment in Ancient Rome*. London: Routledge, 1996.

Becker, Marjorie. *Setting the Virgin on Fire: Lázaro Cárdenas and the Redemption of the Mexican Revolution*. Berkeley: University of California Press, 1995.

Beer, Caroline. "Making Abortion Laws in Mexico: Salience and Autonomy in the Policymaking Process." *Comparative Politics* 50, no. 11 (October 2017): 41–59.

Belausteguigoitia, Marisa. "El aborto en México." *Debate Feminista* 3 (March 1991): 76–81.

Blum, Ann S. *Domestic Economies: Family, Work, and Welfare in Mexico City, 1884–1943*. Lincoln: University of Nebraska Press, 2009.

Boyer, Richard. "Honor among Plebians." In *The Faces of Honor: Sex, Shame, and Violence in Colonial Latin America*, edited by Lyman L. Johnson and Sonya Lipsett-Rivera, 152–78. Albuquerque: University of New Mexico Press, 1998.

Boylan, Kristina A. "Revolutionary and Not-So-Revolutionary Negotiations in Catholic Annulment, Bigamy, and Divorce Trials: The Archdiocese of Mexico, 1929–1940." In *Faith and Piety in Revolutionary Mexico*, edited by Matthew Butler, 167–83. New York: Palgrave Macmillan, 2007.

Breña, Juan. "Juicio crítico del 'Juicio crítico sobre los artículos 569 y 570 del Código Penal vigente.'" *Crónica médica Mexicana* 1, no. 1 (May 1, 1898): 257–324.

Briggs, Gerald G., Roger K. Freeman, and Sumner J. Yaffe. *Drugs in Pregnancy and Lactation*. 8th ed. Philadelphia PA: Wokters Kluwer, 2008.

Buffington, Robert. "Looking Forward, Looking Back: Judicial Discretion and State Legitimation in Modern Mexico." *Crime, Histoire, & Sociétés* 2, no. 2 (1998): 15–34.

Cabrera, Gustavo. "Demographic Dynamics and Development: The Role of Population Policy in Mexico." *Population Development Review* 20 (1994): 105–20.

Calvo, Thomas. "The Warmth of the Hearth: Seventeenth-Century Guadalajara Families." In *Sexuality and Marriage in Colonial Latin America*, edited by Asunción Lavrin, 287–312. Lincoln: University of Nebraska Press, 1990.

Cano, Gabriela. "Una perspectiva del aborto en los años treinta: la propuesta marxista." *Debate Feminista* 2 (September 1990): 362–72.

Cantú, José María, Alejando Hernández, Rafael Alvarez, Julio César Margáin, and Salvador Armendares. "Actitud del médico ante el aborto." *Ginecología y obstetricia de México* 37, no. 223 (May 1975): 275–85.

Catholic Church. *Catecismo para uso de los párrocos, hecho por el IV Concilio Provincial Mexicano*. Mexico City: Lic. D. Josef de Jaúregui, 1772.

———. *A Decree Made at Rome, the Second of March, 1679 Condemning Some Opinions of the Jesuits and Other Casuits*. Accessed February 7, 2024. https://quod.lib.umich.edu/e/eebo2/A45897.0001.001/1:3.2?rgn=div2;view=fulltext.

Cházaro, Laura. "Mexican Women's Pelves and Obstetrical Procedures: Interventions with Forceps in Late Nineteenth-Century Medicine." Translated by Paul Kersey. *Feminist Review* 70 (2005): 100–115.

Christopoulos, John. *Abortion in Early Modern Italy*. Cambridge MA: Harvard University Press, 2021.

Código criminal y penal del estado libre y soberano de Oaxaca expedido por su gobernador constitucional, C. General Félix Diaz. Oaxaca: Impreson por M. Rincon, 1871.

Código penal del estado de Chihuahua. 1987. https://www.cjf.gob.mx/documentos/2011/html /dgdhegyai/tortura/tortura/documentos/punto_ii/ii.8.pdf.

Código penal del estado de Yucatán. Mérida: Imp. Literaria, dirigido por Gil Canto, 1871.

Código penal del estado libre y soberano de Puebla. December 23, 1986. https://armonizacion.cndh .org.mx/Content/Files/LGBTTTI/CodPenal/21codigo_PE_Pue.pdf.

Código penal del estado libre y soberna de Tlaxcala. Tlaxcala: Imprenta del Gobierno del Estado, 1879.

Código penal para el Distrito Federal. Publicada en la Gaceta Oficial del Distrito federal el 16 de julio de 2002. https://www.congresocdmx.gob.mx/media/documentos/9cdocdef5d5adba1c 8e25b34751cccfdcca80e2c.pdf.

Código penal para el Distrito Federal y Territorio de la Baja California sobre delitos del fuero común y para toda la república sobre delitos contra la federación. Mexico City: Imprenta del Gobierno, en Palacio a cargo de José María Sandoval, 1871.

Código penal para el Distrito Federal y Territorio de la Baja California sobre delitos del fuero común y para toda la república sobre delitos contra la federación. Puebla: Imp. de T. F. Neve, 1876.

Cohain, Judy Slome, Rina E. Buxbaum, and David Mankuta. "Spontaneous First-Trimester Miscarriage Rates per Woman among Parous Women with 1 or More Pregnancies of 24 Weeks or More." BMC *Pregnancy Childbirth* 17, no. 437 (2017): 1–7.

Concilio III Provincial Mexicano, celebrado en México el año de 1585. Mexico City: Mariano Galvan Rivera, 1859.

Cook, Rebecca J., Joanna Erdman, and Bernard M. Dickens, eds. *Abortion Law in Transnational Perspective*. Philadelphia: University of Pennsylvania Press, 2014.

Cosminsky, Sheila. *Midwives and Mothers: The Medicalization of Childbirth on a Guatemalan Plantation*. Austin: University of Texas Press, 2016.

Cruz, David. *¿Existen indicaciones formales para provocar el aborto? Tesis inaugural*. Mexico City: Talleres de la Tipografia del Hospicio, 1897.

Dayton, Cornelia Hughes. "Taking the Trade: Abortion and Gender Relations in an Eighteenth-Century New England Village." *William and Mary Quarterly* 48, no. 1 (January 1991): 19–49.

"Decreto por el que se reforma el Código Penal para el Distrito Federal y se adiciona a la Ley de Salud para el Distrito Federal." *Gaceta Oficial del Distrito Federal*, April 26, 2007. https:// www.semujeres.cdmx.gob.mx/storage/app/media/ILE/Decreto.pdf.

Diccionario de ciencias eclesiásticas. Vol. 1. Madrid: Liberia Católica é Imprenta de San José, 1883.

Dore, Elizabeth. "One Step Forward, Two Steps Back: Gender and the State in the Long Nineteenth Century." In *Hidden Histories of Gender and the State in Latin America,* edited by Elizabeth Dore and Maxine Moyneux, 2–32. Durham NC: Duke University Press, 2000.

Dublán, Manuel, and José María Lozano, eds. *Legislación Mexicana. Colección completa de las disposiciones legislativas expedidas desde la independencia de la república.* Tomo 6. Mexico City: Imprenta del Comercio, de Dublán y Chávez, 1877.

Dueñas Vargas, Guiomar. "Infanticidio y aborto en la colonia: pócimas de ruda y cocimiento de mastranto." *En otras palabras* 1 (July–December 1996): 43–48.

Duque de Estrada, Juan. "Aborto Provocado." *Crónica médica Mexicana* 1, no. 8 (February 1, 1898): 173–75.

———. "La embriotomía en la casa de maternidad de México." *Crónica médica Mexicana* 1, no. 2 (August 1, 1897): 32–36.

Emmart, Emily Walcott. *The Badianus Manuscript (Codex Barberini, Latin 241) Vatican Library: An Aztec Herbal of 1552.* Baltimore MD: Johns Hopkins University Press, 1940.

Encisco Rojas, Dolores. "'Mal parir,' 'parir fuera del tiempo' o 'aborto procurado y efectuado.' Su penalización en Nueva España y en el México independiente." *Dimensión Antropológica* 17, no. 49 (May–August 2010): 91–123.

Erviti, Joaquina. *El aborto entre mujeres pobres.* Cuernavaca: Centro Regional de Investigaciones Multidisciplinarias, Universidad Nacional Autónoma de México, 2005.

Erviti, Joaquina, Roberto Castro, and Itzel A Sosa Sánchez. "Las luchas clasificatorias en torno al aborto: el caso de los médicos en hospitales públicos de México." *Estudios sociológicos* 24, no. 72 (2006): 637–65.

Escontria, Manuel. "La Eugenesia y la Limitación de Natalidad." *Gaceta médica de México* 61, no. 7 (July 1 1930): 414–22.

Escriche y Martín, Joaquin. *Diccionario razonado de legislación y jurisprudencia.* Madrid: Viuda e hijos de A. Calleja, 1847.

———. *Diccionario razonado de legislación y jurisprudencia.* Paris: Librería de Rosay, Bouret y Compania, 1854.

Espinosa Tavares, Martha Liliana. "'They Are Coming in So Fast That If We Had Publicity about the Clinic We Would Be Swamped': Edris Rice-Wray, the First Family Planning Clinic in Mexico (1959), and the Intervention of US-Based Private Foundations." *Journal of Women's History* 34, no. 2 (2022): 76–96.

Federici, Silvia. *Caliban and the Witch: Women, the Body, and Primitive Accumulation.* New York: Autonomedia, 2014.

Ferreira, Mercedes B. "Problemas legales del transplante de embrión como alternativa al aborto." *Fem* 16, no. 109 (1992–93): 13–15.

Few, Martha. "Medical *Mestizaje* and the Politics of Pregnancy in Colonial Guatemala." In *Science in the Spanish and Portuguese Empires, 1500–1800*, edited by Daniela Bleichmar, Paula De Vos, Kristin Huffine, and Kevin Sheehan, 132–46. Stanford CA: Stanford University Press, 2008.

Few, Martha, Zeb Tortorici, Adam Warren, eds. *Baptism through Incision.* Translated by Nina M. Scott. University Park: Penn State University Press, 2020.

Foppa, Alaíde, and Helene F. de Aguilar. "The First Feminist Congress in Mexico, 1916." *Signs* 5, no. 1 (Autumn 1979): 192–99.

French, William E. *The Heart in a Glass Jar: Love Letters, Bodies, and the Law in Mexico.* Lincoln: University of Nebraska Press, 2015.

Galindo, Hermila. "La Mujer en el Porvenir." Primero Congreso Feminista de Yucatán, January 1916. https://ideasfem.wordpress.com/textos/f/f13/.

García Goyena, Florencio, and Joaquín Aguirre. *Febrero, ó librería de jueces, abogados, y escribanos, comprensiva de los códigos civil, criminal, y administrativo.* Madrid: I Roix, 1842.

Garza, James. *The Imagined Underworld: Sex, Crime, and Vice in Porfirian Mexico City.* Lincoln: University of Nebraska Press, 2007.

Gastélum, Bernardo J. "¿Es el aborto provocado un recurso terapéutico?" *Gaceta médica de México* 89, no. 5 (May 1959): 451–58.

———. "Tratamiento del aborto irremediable de los tres primeros meses." *La revista médica de Yucatán* 17, no. 12 (June 30, 1934): 541–49.

Gobierno del Estado de Puebla. *Código penal del estado libre y soberano de Puebla.* Accessed December 29, 2023. https://ojp.puebla.gob.mx/legislacion-del-estado/item/375-codigo -penal-del-estado-libre-y-soberano-de-puebla.

Gómez, José. *Tratamiento del aborto.* Coatepec: Imprenta de A. M. Rebolledo, 1895.

Gonzalbo Aizpuru, Pilar. "Familia y convivencia en la ciudad de México a fines del siglo XVIII." In *Familias iberoamericanas. Historia, identidad y conflictos*, edited by Pilar Gonzalbo Aizpuru, 163–78. Mexico City: Grijalbo, 2001.

Gonzáles de León Aguirre, Deyanira, and Addis Abeba Salinas Urbina. "Los médicos en formación y el aborto: Opinión de estudiantes de medicina en la Ciudad de México." *Cuadernos de Saúde Pública* 13, no. 2 (April 1997): 227–36.

Gonzáles Santos, Sandra P. *A Portrait of Assisted Reproduction in Mexico: Scientific, Political, and Cultural Interactions.* Cham, Switzerland: Palgrave Macmillan, 2020.

González M., Lucero. "La penalización del aborto en México." *Política y Cultura* 1 (Fall 1992): 49–55.

González Mariscal, Olga Islas de. "Evolución del aborto en México." *Boletín de Derecho Comparado* 41, no. 123 (September–December 2008): 1313–41.

Grupo de Información en Reproducción Elegida (GIRE). *Maternidad o castigo: La criminalización del aborto en México.* Mexico City: GIRE, 2018.

———. *Omission and Indifference: Reproductive Rights in Mexico*. Mexico City: GIRE, 2013.

Hernández, Francisco. *Qvatro libros de la naturaleza y virtudes de las plantas, y animales que están recevidos en el vso de Medicina en la Nueva España, y la Methodo, y correccion y preparacion, que para administrarllas se requiere con lo que el doctor Francisco Hernandez escriuio en lengua Latina. Traduzido, y aumentados mucho simples, y Compuestos y otros muchos secretos curativos, por Fr. Francisco Ximenez.* Mexico City: Casa de la Viuda de Diego Lopez Daualos, 1615.

Herrasti, Alicia. "Algunos Mitos y Realidades sobre ABORTO." Mexico City: El Verdadero Catolicismo, 2001.

Hidalgo y Carpio, Luis. "Jurisprudencia Médica." *Gaceta médica de México* 2, no. 19 (October 1, 1865): 298–301.

Hidalgo y Carpio, Luis, and Gustavo Ruiz y Sandoval. *Compendio de medicina legal arreglado a la legislación del distrito federal.* Vol. 1. Mexico City: Imprenta de Ignacion Esclante, 1877.

Holler, Jacqueline. "Mixing/Medicines: Healing Exchanges among Women in Early Colonial New Spain (1530–1650)." *Gender and History* 33, no. 3 (July 2021): 1–20.

Huacuja, Francisco. *Tratado práctico de partos que comprende las nociones más precisas sobre los accidentes y obstaculos que presentan y el reglamento de que habla la ley 2 de marzo de 1852.* Morelia: O. Ortiz, 1857.

Ibáñez, Joaquín. *Someras reflexiones sobre el aborto obstetrical, el parto prematuro y la gastrohisterotomía.* Puebla: Imp. De Ibáñez y Lamarque, 1882.

Ibarra, Rodolfo J. *Tratamiento de las complicaciones del aborto. Tesis inaugural.* Mexico City: Oficina Tip. De la Secretaría de fomento, 1898.

Inter-American Commission on Human Rights. "Report No. 21/7. Petition 161-02. Friendly Settlement Paulina del Carmen Ramírez Jacinto." March 9, 2007. https://www.cidh.oas.org /annualrep/2007eng/Mexico161.02eng.htm.

Jaffary, Nora E. *False Mystics: Deviant Orthodoxy in Colonial Mexico.* Lincoln: University of Nebraska Press, 2004.

———. "Maternity and Morality in Puebla's Nineteenth-Century Infanticide Trials." *Law and History Review* 39, no. 2 (June 2021): 299–319.

———. "Medicine, Midwifery, and the Law: Views of Infanticide and Abortion in the Yucatán, 1840–1910." *Mexican Studies/Estudios Mexicanos* 37, no. 1 (Winter 2021): 61–92.

———, ed. "A Midwife Accused of Abortion, Yucatán (1853)." HOSLAC—History of Science in Latin America and the Caribbean. Accessed February 7, 2024. https://mypages.unh.edu /hoslac/book/sulu-abortion.

———. *Reproduction and Its Discontents in Mexico: Childbirth and Contraception from 1750 to 1905.* Chapel Hill: University of North Carolina Press, 2016.

Jaffary, Nora E., and Jane E. Mangan. "Isabel Hernández, Midwife and Healer, Appears before the Inquisition (Mexico, 1652)." In *Women in Colonial Latin America 1526 to 1806: Texts and Contexts,* edited by Nora E. Jaffary and Jane E. Mangan, 128–44. Indianapolis: Hackett, 2018.

Jelen, Ted G., Danielle Roth-Johnson, and John P. Tuman. "Culture Wars in Latin America: Religious Attitudes toward Homosexuality and Abortion in Four Countries." *Journal of Religion and Theology* 1, no. 1 (2017): 1–7.

Jiménez Huerta, Mariano. "Delito de infanticidio." *Criminalia* 25, no. 2 (February 1959): 106–20.

Juárez, Fatima, Susheela Singh, Isaac Maddow-Zimet, and Deirdre Wulf. *Unintended Pregnancy and Induced Abortion in Mexico: Causes and Consequences.* New York: Guttmacher Institute, 2013.

Juárez, Fatima, Shusheela Singh, Sandra G. García, and Claudia Diaz Olavarrieta. "Estimates of Induced Abortion in Mexico: What's Changed between 1990 and 2006?" *International Perspectives on Sexual and Reproductive Health* 34, no. 4 (December 2008): 158–68.

Knight, Alan. *The Mexican Revolution.* 2 vols. Cambridge: Cambridge University Press, 1986.

Koblitz, Ann Hibner. *Sex and Herbs and Birth Control: Women and Fertility Regulation through the Ages.* Seattle WA: Kovalevskaia Fund, 2014.

Lamas, Marta. "The Feminist Movement and the Development of a Political Discourse on Voluntary Motherhood." *Reproductive Health Matters* 5, no. 10 (November 1997): 58–67.

———. "La despenalización del aborto en México." *Nueva Sociedad* 220 (March–April 2009): 154–72.

———. *La interrupción legal del embarazo: El caso de la Ciudad de México.* Mexico City: Fondo de la Cultura Económica, Universidad Nacional Autónoma de México, 2017.

Lamas, Marta, and Sharon Bisell. "Abortion and Politics in Mexico: 'Context is All.'" *Reproductive Health Matters: An International Journal on Sexual and Reproductive Health and Rights* 8, no. 16 (November 2000): 10–23.

Lavrin, Asunción. "Introduction: The Scenario, the Actors, and the Issues." In *Sexuality and Marriage in Colonial Latin America*, edited by Asunción Lavrin, 1–43. Lincoln: University of Nebraska Press, 1989.

Lipsett Rivera, Sonya. *Gender and the Negotiation of Daily Life in Mexico, 1750–1856.* Lincoln: University of Nebraska Press, 2012.

———. *The Origins of Macho: Men and Masculinity in Colonial Mexico.* Albuquerque: University of New Mexico Press, 2019.

Loeza, Soledad. "La iglesia y la educación en México. Una historia en episodios." In *Historia y nación (actas del Congreso en homenaje a Josefina Zoraida Vázquez): 1. Historia de la educación y enseñanza de la historia*, edited by Pilar Gonzalbo Aizpuru, 173–93. Mexico City: El Colegio de México, 1998.

López, Gregorio. *Las Siete Partidas del sabio rey don Alonso el Nono. Glosadas por el Licenciado Gregorio Lopez. Tercera Partida.* Salamanca: Andrea de Portonaris, 1555.

———. *Las Siete Partidas del sabio rey don Alonso el Nono, nueuamente glosadas por Gregorio Lopez. Séptima Partida.* Valladolid: Diego Fernandez de Cordova, 1587.

López Hermosa, Alberto. *Aborto en sus relaciones con la legislación penal.* Mexico City: Tip. Economía, 1903.

———. "Medicina legal: Juicio crítico sobre los arts. 569 y 570 del Código Penal vigente." *Gaceta médica de México* 34, no. 7 (April 1 1897): 189–206.

López Sánchez, Oliva. "La centralidad del útero y sus anexos en las representaciones técnicas del cuerpo femenino en la medicina del siglo XIX." In *Enjaular los cuerpos: Normativas decimonónicas y feminidad en México*, edited by Julia Tuñon, 146–84. Mexico City: El Colegio de México, 2008.

Lucero, Bonnie. *Race and Reproduction in Cuba*. Athens: University of Georgia Press, 2022.

Lumbier, Raimundo. *Noticia de las sesenta y cinco proposiciones nuevamente condenadas por N. SS. P. Inocencio XI mediante su Decreto de 2 de Mayo del año de 1679*. Mexico City: Juan de Ribera, 1684.

Madrazo, Alejandro. "The Evolution of Mexico City's Abortion Laws: From Public Morality to Women's Autonomy." *International Journal of Gynecology and Obstetrics* 106 (2009): 266–69.

———. "Narratives of Prenatal Personhood in Abortion Law." In *Abortion Law in Transnational Perspective*, edited by Rebecca J, Cook, Joanna Erdman, and Bernard M. Dickens, 327–46. Philadelphia: University of Pennsylvania Press, 2014.

Maier, Elizabeth. "Documenting Mexico's Culture War." *Latin American Perspectives* 39, no. 6 (November 2012): 155–64.

———. "La disputa sobre el aborto en México: Discursos contrastados de personificación, derechos, la familia y el Estado." *Revista Gerencia y Políticas de Salud* 14, no. 29 (2015): 10–24.

Marin, Rubén. "Sobre la legislación del aborto." *Sugestiones* 12, no. 138 (February 1947): 106–10.

Márquez Murrieta, Alicia. "Aborto y derechos reproductivos: Leyes y debates públicos." In *Los grandes problemas de México: Vol. 8, Relaciones de género*, edited by Ana María Tepichin, Karine Tinat, and Luzelena Gutiérrez, 179–200. Mexico City: El Colegio de México, 2010.

Martinez, José G. "Contribución al Estudio de la Supresión del llamado 'Aborto Terapéutico.'" *Ginecología y obstetricia de México* 7, no. 4 (July–August 1952): 258–61.

Martínez de Castro, Antonio. *Exposición de motivos del código penal vigente en el Distrito Federal y territorio de la Baja California*. Mexico City: Imprenta de Francisco Díaz de León, 1876.

Marván, Alcibiádes. "¿Es el aborto provocado un recurso terapéutico? Comentario al trabajo del Dr. Bernardo Gastellum." *Gaceta médica de México* 89, no. 5 (May 1959): 459–61.

Mauriceau, François. *Traité des maladies des femmes grosses, et de celles qui sont nouvellement accouchées*. Paris: n.p., 1675.

Mayer, Óscar J. *El aspecto médico-legal del aborto*. Tesis de Medicina. Mexico City: Escuela Nacional de Medicina, 1908.

McCaa, Robert. "The Peopling of Nineteenth-Century Mexico: Critical Scrutiny of a Censured Century." In *Statistical Abstract of Latin America*, vol. 30, part 1, edited by James W. Wilkie, Carlos Alberto Contreras, and Christof Anders Weber, 602–33. Los Angeles: UCLA Latin American Center, University of California, 1993.

McEnroe, Sean F. *From Colony to Nationhood in Mexico: Laying the Foundations, 1560–1840*. Cambridge: Cambridge University Press, 2012.

Menocal, Francisco. *Estudio sobre el aborto en México*. Mexico City: Imp. de J. M. Lara, 1869.

Molina, Alonso de. *Confesionario mayor en la Lengua Mexicana y Castellana* (1569). 5th ed. México: Universidad Nacional Autónoma de México, Instituto de Investigaciones Filológicas, 1984.

Monlau, Pedro Felipe. *El libro de los casados*. Madrid: Imprenta y Esterotipia de M. Rivadeneyra, 1865.

Monsiváis, Carlos. "Foreword. When Gender Can't Be Seen amid the Symbols: Women and the Mexican Revolution." In *Sex in Revolution: Gender, Politics, and Power in Modern Mexico*, edited by Jocelyn Olcott, Mary Vaughan, and Gabriela Cano, 1–20. Durham NC: Duke University Press, 2006.

Narvaez, Fernando. "Interrupción terapéutica del embarazo por el método de Boero." *Revista médica de Yucatán* 22, no. 5 (June 30, 1943): 89–93.

Navarro y Cardona, Eduardo. *Del parto prematuro en México y de las maneras con que se le ha provocado. Tesis Inaugural*. Mexico City: Imprenta de Diáz de León y White, 1873.

Nelson, Jennifer. "Feminism, Human Rights, and Abortion Debates in Mexico." *Journal of Women's History* 34, no. 2 (Summer 2022): 119–40.

Nieto de Piña, Cristóbal. *Instruccion medica para discernir, si el feto muerto, lo ha sido dentro o fuera de el útero*. Sevilla: Imprenta de Manuel Nicolas Vazquez, n.d.

Nigenda, Gustavo, and Amrando Solórzano. "Doctors and Corporatist Politics: The Case of the Mexican Medical Profession." *Journal of Health, Politics, Policy, and Law* 22, no. 1 (February 1997): 73–99.

Noonan, John T. "Abortion and the Catholic Church: A Summary History." *Natural Law Forum*, Paper 126 (1967): 85–131. http://scholarship.law.nd.edu/nd_naturallaw_forum/126.

Núñez, B. Fernanda. "Imaginario médico y práctica jurídica en torno al aborto durante el último tercio del siglo XIX." In *Curar, sanar, y educar: Enfermedad y sociedad en México siglos XIX y XX*, edited by Claudia Agostoni, 127–62. Mexico City: IIH-UNAM, 2008.

Núñez Cetina, Saydi. "Reforma social, honor y justicia: infanticidio y aborto en la Ciudad de México, 1920–1940." *Signos Históricos* 28 (2012): 68–113.

O'Brien, Elizabeth. "Intimate Interventions: The Cultural Politics of Reproductive Surgery in Mexico, 1790–1940." PhD diss., University of Texas at Austin, 2019.

———. "The Many Meanings of *Aborto*: Pregnancy Termination and the Instability of a Medical Category over Time." *Women's History Review* 30, no. 6 (2021): 952–70.

———. *Surgery and Salvation: Religion, Racism, and Reproduction in Mexico, 1745–1940*. Chapel Hill: University of North Carolina Press, 2023.

———. "'A Tacit Pact with the State': Constrained Choice and the Politics of Revolution in 1930s Mexico." *Journal of Women's History* 34, no. 2 (Summer 2022): 53–75.

Ojeda Velázquez, Jorge. "Aborto, iglesia, sociedad y Estado." *Criminalia Año XLLLVII Nueva época*, December 2020, 171–96.

Olcott, Jocelyn, Mary Kay Vaughan, and Gabriela Cano. *Sex in Revolution: Gender, Politics, and Power in Modern Mexico*. Durham NC: Duke University Press, 2006.

Opperman, Stephanie Baker. "'There Was No "Family Planning Movement," There Was Just Us': The Associación Pro-Salud Maternal and Birth Control in 1960s Mexico." *Journal of Women's History* 34, no. 2 (2022): 97–118.

Ornelas Méndez, Candy E. *Inventario del Archivo Histórico de la Unión Nacional de Padres de Familia, Ciudad de México*. Mexico City: Adabi, 2017.

Ortiz-Ortega, Adriana. "Entrevista a Luis de la Barreda." In *Razones y pasiones en torno al aborto*, edited by Adriana Ortiz-Ortega, 32–33. Mexico City: Edamex, 1994.

———. "The Feminist Demand for Legal Abortion: A Disruption of the Mexican State and Catholic Church Relations (1871–1995)." PhD diss., Yale University, 1996.

———. "Law and the Politics of Abortion." In *Decoding Gender: Law and Practice in Contemporary Mexico*, edited by Helga Battenmann, Victoria Chenaut, and Ann Varley, 197–212. New Brunswick NJ: Rutgers University Press, 2007.

———. "The Politics of Abortion in Mexico: The Paradox of Doble Discurso." In *Where Human Rights Begin: Health, Sexuality, and Women*, edited by Wendy Chavkin and Ellen Chesler, 154–79. New Brunswick NJ: Rutgers University Press, 2005.

Overmyer-Velázquez, Mark. *Visions of the Emerald City: Modernity, Tradition, and the Formation of Porfirian Mexico*. Durham NC: Duke University Press, 2008.

Owensby, Brian. *Empire of Law and Justice in Colonial Mexico*. Stanford CA: Stanford University Press, 2008.

Pavón Vasconcelos, Francisco H. "El delito de aborto." *Criminalia* 25, no. 2 (July–December 1959): 594–604.

Perera Castillo, Fernando. "Lugar de la cirugía en el aborto" (1951). *Ginecología y obstetricia de México* 74 (2006): 394–97.

Pérez Duarte y N., Alicia Elena. "El aborto en nuestra república." In *Razones y pasiones en torno al aborto: una contribución al debate*, edited by Adriana Ortiz-Ortega, 34–40. Mexico City: EdaMex, 1994.

Pérez Molina, Augusto, Manuel Díaz Estua, and Abraham Bazán. "Consideraciones sobre el aborto terapéutico." *Ginecología y obstetricia de México* 7, no. 4 (July–August 1952): 251–57.

Pius Episcopus Servorum Dei ad Perpetuam Re Momoriam. "Constitutio SS. D. N. PII PP. IX, Qua Numerus Censuraum Latae Sententiae Restringitur." In *Elements of Ecclesiastical Law*, vol. 1, 9th ed., edited by S. B. Smith, D.D., 536–44. New York: Benziger Brothers, 1887.

Porter, Susie S. *From Angel to Office Worker: Middle-Class Identity and Female Consciousness in Mexico, 1890–1950*. Lincoln: University of Nebraska Press, 2018.

Premo, Bianca. *The Enlightenment on Trial: Ordinary Litigants and Colonialism in the Spanish Empire.* New York: Oxford University Press, 2017.

"Programas para la Escuela Nacional de Medecina." *Revista de la instrucción pública Mexicana* 4, no. 17 (November 1, 1900): 499–510.

Quezada, Noémi. "Creencias tradicionales sobre embarazo y parto." *Anales de antropología* 14, no. 1 (1977): 307–26.

———. "Métodos anticonceptivos y abortivos tradicionales." *Anales de antropología* 12, no. 1 (1975): 223–42.

Real Academia Española. *Fuero juzgo en Latin y Castellano cotejado con los más antiguos y precisos códices por La Real Academia Española.* Madrid: Ibarra, 1815.

"Reglamento y Arancel del Consejo Médico-Legal." *Gaceta médica de México* 16, no. 18 (July 1, 1881): 225–28.

Riddle, John M. *Contraception and Abortion from the Ancient World to the Renaissance.* Cambridge MA: Harvard University Press, 1992.

Rivera Reynaldos, Lisette Griselda. "Crímenes pasionales y relaciones de género en México, 1880–1910." *Nuevo Mundo, Mundos Nuevos,* Colloques, November 19, 2006. http://journals.openedition.org/nuevomundo/2835.

Roa Bárcena, Rafael. *Manual razonado de práctica criminal y médico-legal forense mexicana: Obra escrita con arreglo a las leyes antiguas y modernas vigentes, y a las doctrinas de los mejores autores, bajo un plan nuevo y al alcance de todos.* Mexico City: Imp. De Andrade y Escalante, 1860.

Rodríguez, Juan María. *Guía clínica del arte de los partos.* Mexico City: Imprenta de Ignacio Escalante, 1878.

Rodríguez O., Jaime E. *"We Are Now the True Spaniards": Sovereignty, Revolution, Independence, and the Emergence of the Federal Republic of Mexico, 1808–1824.* Stanford CA: Stanford University Press, 2012.

Rodríguez Raygoza, Elizabeth. "¿Víctimas o victimarias? Infanticidio y conducta criminal en Jalisco, 1867–1873." Tesis de Maestría en Historia, Instituto José Ma. Luis Mora, 2004.

Roys, Ralph L. *The Ethnobotany of the Maya.* New Orleans LA: Tulane University Press, 1931.

Saavedra, Alfredo. "El Aborto Criminal y la Eugenesia." *Criminalia* 4 (June 1938): 624–28.

Sahagún, Bernardino de. *Historia general de las cosas de Nueva España.* Mexico City: Cien de México, 2000.

Sánchez-Rivera, R. "The Making of 'La Gran Familia Mexicana': Eugenics, Gender, and Sexuality in Mexico." *Journal of Historical Sociology* 34 (2021): 161–85.

Sanders, Nichole S. *Gender and Welfare in Mexico: The Consolidation of a Postrevolutionary State.* University Park: Penn State University Press, 2011.

———. "Gender and Welfare Reform in Post-Revolutionary Mexico." *Gender and History* 20, no. 1 (April 2008): 170–75.

———. "Women, Sex, and the 1950s Acción Católica's Campaña Nacional de Moralización del Ambiente." *Mexican Studies* 36, no. 1 (Winter–Summer 2020): 270–97.

Sanger, Margarita. "La regulación de la natalidad o la brújula del hogar. Medios seguros y científicos para evitar la concepción." Mérida, 1922. https://sangerpapers.files.wordpress.com /2016/01/la-brc3bajula-del-hogar.pdf.

Santillán, Martha Esqueda. *Delincuencia femenina: Ciudad de México 1940–1954*. Mexico City: Instituto Mora, Instituto Nacional de Ciencias Penales, 2017.

———. "Maternidad y transgresiones penales en el Distrito Federal, 1940–1950." *Historia Mexicana* 68, no. 3 (2019): 1121–64.

———. *Mujeres criminales. Entre la ley y la justicia*. Mexico City: Crítica, 2021.

Scardaville, Michael C. "(Hapsburg) Law and (Bourbon) Order: State Authority, Popular Unrest, and the Criminal Justice System in Bourbon Mexico City." *Americas* 50, no. 4 (1994): 501–25.

Schell, Patience A. "Gender, Class, and Anxiety at the Gabriel Mistral Vocational School, Revolutionary Mexico City." In *Sex in Revolution: Gender, Politics, and Power in Modern Mexico*, edited by Jocelyn Olcott, Mary Kay Vaughan, and Gabriela Cano, 112–26. Durham NC: Duke University Press, 2006.

Schiebinger, Londa. *Plants and Empire: Colonial Bioprospecting in the Atlantic World*. Cambridge MA: Harvard University Press, 2004.

Secretaria de Gobernación. *Código penal para el distrito y territorios federales*. Mexico City: Talleres Gráficos de la Nación, 1929.

———. *Código penal para el distrito y territorios federales en materia de fuero común, y para toda la República en material de fuero federal*. Mexico City: Talleres Gráficos de la Nación, 1931.

Secretaría de Salud. "Norma Oficial Mexicana NOM-046-SSA2-2005. Violencia familiar, sexual y contra las mujeres. Criterios para la prevención y atención." April 16, 2009. Last updated March 24, 2016. https://www.cndh.org.mx/sites/default/files/doc/Programas /VIH/LeyesNormasReglamentos/NormaOficialMexicana/NOM-046-SSA2-2005 _ViolenciaFamiliarSexual.pdf.

Segura, Ignacio. *Avisos saludables a las parteras para el cumplimiento de su obligación. Sacados de la "Emriología Sacra" del Sr. Dr. D. Francisco Manuel Cangliamila, y puestos en castellano por el Dr. D. Ignacio Segura, Médico de esta corte*. Mexico City: F. de Zúñiga y Ontiveros, 1775.

Serrano Limón, Luis Francisco. *Aborto en México. ¿Crisis o Solución?* Mexico: Promesa, 1983.

Shelton, Laura. "Birth and Death in the Maternity Ward of Guadalajara's Hospital Civil, 1888–1940." *Journal of Women's History* 34, no. 2 (Summer 2022): 31–52.

———. *For Tranquility and Order: Family and Community on Mexico's Northern Frontier, 1800–1850*. Tucson: University of Arizona Press, 2010.

———. "Infanticidio y disciplina popular en el sistema judicial de Sonora, México, entre 1855 y 1919." *Culturales* 1, no. 11 (January–June 2017): 255–98.

Singer, Elyse Ona. *Lawful Sins: Abortion Rights and Reproductive Governance in Mexico*. Stanford CA: Stanford University Press, 2022.

Sloan, Kathryn A. *Runaway Daughters: Seduction, Elopement, and Honor in Nineteenth-Century Mexico*. Albuquerque: University of New Mexico Press, 2008.

Smithe, J. A. "Breve estudio médico-jurídico sobre el aborto." *Criminalia* 7, no. 4 (1945): 609–20.

Speckman Guerra, Elisa. *Crimen y castigo: Legislación penal, interpretaciones de la criminalidad y administración de justicia (Ciudad de México, 1872–1910)*. Mexico City: El Colegio de México, Universidad Nacional Autónoma de México, 2002.

———. "Disorder and Control: Crime, Justice, and Punishment in Porfirian and Revolutionary Society." In *A Companion to Mexican History and Culture*, edited by William H. Beezley, 371–89. Chichester, West Sussex: Wiley-Blackwell, 2011.

———. "Morir a manos de una mujer: Homicidas e infanticidas en el porfiriato." In *Disidenica y disidentes en la historia de México*, edited by Felipe Castro Gutiérrez and Marcela Terrazas, 295–320. Mexico City: Universidad Nacional Autónoma de México, 2003.

Spivack, Carla. "To Bring Down the Flowers: The Cultural Context of Abortion Law in Early Modern England." *William and Mary Quarterly* 107 (2007): 107–51.

Stein, Rob. "Embryo Research to Reduce the Need for In Vitro Fertilization Raises Ethical Concerns." NPR, January 15, 2020. https://www.npr.org/sections/health-shots/2020/01/15/796018096/embryo-research-to-reduce-need-for-in-vitro-fertilization-raises-ethical-concern.

Stern, Alexandra Minna. "'The Hour of Eugenics' in Veracruz, Mexico: Radical Politics, Public Health, and Latin America's Only Sterilization Law." *Hispanic American Historical Review* 91, no. 3 (2011): 431–43.

Stevenson, Linda. "Gender Politics and Policy Process in Mexico, 1968–2000: Symbolic Gains for Women in an Emerging Democracy." PhD diss., University of Pittsburgh, 2000.

Suárez y Lopez-Guazo, Laura. "The Mexican Eugenics Society: Racial Selection and Improvement." In *The Reception of Darwinism in the Iberian World: Spain, Spanish American and Brazil*, edited by Thomas F. Glick, Miguel Angel Puig-Samper, and Rosaura Ruiz, 143–52. London: Kluwer, 2001.

Suprema Corte de Justicia de la Nación. "Mexican Supreme Court: Landmark Decisions at the Vanguard for Reproductive Rights World Wide." Comunicados de Prensa, no. 298 (October 1, 2021). https://www.internet2.scjn.gob.mx/red2/comunicados/noticia.asp?id=6606.

———. "Suprema Corte declara inconstitucional la criminalización total del aborto." Comunicados de Prensa, no. 271 (September 7, 2021). https://www.internet2.scjn.gob.mx/red2/comunicados/noticia.asp?id=6579.

Tajonar y Cardosa, Jesús. *Breve estudio comparativo entre la embriotomía y la operación cesárea*. Mexico City: Imp. Berrueco Hnos., 1884.

Tanck de Estrada, Dorothy. "Muerte Precoz. Los niños en el siglo XVIII." In *Historia de la vida cotidiana en México vol. III: El siglo XVIII. Entre tradición y cambio*, edited by Pilar

Gonzalbo Aizpuru, 213–45. Mexico City: El Colegio de México y el Fondo de Cultura Económica, 2005.

Tarrés, María Luisa. "El movimiento de mujeres y el sistema político mexicano: análisis de la liberalización del aborto, 1976–1990." *Estudios sociológicos* 11, no. 2 (May–August 1993): 365–97.

Torre, Rafael de la. *Ensayo de estudios sobre uno de los problemas médico-legales a que da lugar el aborto. Tesis de Medicina.* Mexico City: Escuela Nacional de Medicina, 1910.

Toxqui, Áurea. "Breadwinners or Entrepreneurs: Women's Involvement in the *Pulquería* World of Mexico City, 1850–1910." In *Alcohol in Latin America: A Social and Cultural History*, edited by Gretchen Pierce and Áurea Toxqui, 104–30. Tucson: University of Arizona Press, 2014.

Trens Marentes, Manuel B. *Estudio de las complicaciones del aborto y su tratamiento.* Mexico City: La Prensa, 1920.

Troconis y Alcalá, Luis. *En los embarazos tiernos, cuál es el mejor procedimiento operatorio para efectuar la desocupación de la matriz?* Mexico City: Imprenta de Francisco Díaz de León, 1885.

Tuman, John P., Danielle Roth-Johnson, and Ted Jelen. "Conscience and Context: Attitudes Toward Abortion in Mexico." *Social Science Quarterly* 94, no. 1 (March 2013): 100–112.

Tutino, John. *Mexico City, 1808: Power, Sovereignty, and Silver in an Age of War and Revolution.* Albuquerque: University of New Mexico Press, 2018.

Twinam, Ann. *Public Lives, Private Secrets: Gender, Honor, and Illegitimacy in Colonial Spanish America.* Stanford CA: Stanford University Press, 1999.

Urías Horcasitas, Beatriz. "Eugenesia y aborto en México (1920–1940)." *Debate Feminista* 27 (April 2003): 305–23.

Uribe-Uran, Victor. *Fatal Love: Spousal Killers, Law, and Punishment in the Late Colonial Spanish Atlantic.* Stanford CA: Stanford University Press, 2016.

Van Dyke, Christina. "Review of *Aquinas on the Beginning and End of Human Life* by Fabrizio Amerini." *Notre Dame Philosophical Reviews*, June 31, 2014. https://ndpr.nd.edu/reviews /aquinas-on-the-beginning-and-end-of-human-life/#:~:text=Aquinas%20holds%20that %20human%20life,to%20as%20%E2%80%98immediate%20hominization%E2%80%99.

Vela, Estafanía. "Current Abortion Regulation in Mexico." *Documentos de Trabajo del CIDE* 50 (2010): 1–19. http://mobile.repositoriodigital.cide.edu/bitstream/handle/11651/1317 /103275.pdf?sequence=1&isAllowed=y.

Venegas, Juan Manuel. *Compendio de la medicina: Ó medicina practica, en que se declara lacónicamente lo mas útil de ella, que el Autor tiene observado en estas Regiones de Nueva España, para casi todas las Enfermedades que acomete al cuerpo humano: Dispuesto en forma alfabetica por el Br. Don Juan Manuel Venegas.* Mexico City: D. Felipe de Zúñiga y Ontiveros, 1788.

Viesca Benavides, Enrique, Salvador de Lara, and Jesús Valdes Muriel. "Consideraciones Sociales y Legales Sobre el Aborto." *Ginecología y obstetricia de México* 5, no. 3 (May–June 1950): 181–95.

Villalobos Quijano, Waldo. *Aborto médico.* Mexico City: Imp. Garmboa, Guzmán, 1902.

Williams, Raymond. *The Country and the City.* New York: Oxford University Press, 1973.

Wilson, Kate S., Sandra G. García, Claudia Díaz Olavarrieta, Aremis Villalobos-Hernández, Jorge Valencia Rodríguez, Patricio Sanhueza Smith, and Courtney Burks. "Public Opinion on Abortion in Mexico City after the Landmark Reform." *Studies in Family Planning* 42, no. 3 (September 2011): 175–82.

Womack, John. *Zapata and the Mexican Revolution*. New York: Vintage, [1968] 1970.

Ximeno, José. *Opúsculo sobre los catorce casos reservados y otras tantas excomuniones sinodales del Concilio Mexicano Provincia tercero celebrado en el año 1585*. Mexico City: Don Alexandro Valdés, 1816.

Zahler, Reuben. "Reforming Women, Protecting Men: The Prosecution of Infanticide in Venezuela's Early Republic, 1820–1860." *Law and History Review* 40, no. 3 (August 2022): 459–89.

INDEX

medical cause for abortion, 76–80, 97–98, 118

medical education, 77–79, 99, 100

medical profession, 98, 118. *See also* doctors; medical students

medical students, 11, 77, 100. *See also* medical education

medicinal abortions, 27, 34–36, 38–39, 59, in the Porfiriato, 63, 75; in the twentieth century, 84, 100. See also *altamisa; cihuapatli; juniper, mifepristone, misoprostol*

medicine, 37–38. *See also* doctors; Mayan medicine; medical students; pre-Columbian medicine; surgical abortions

Medina, Antonio, 21, 23, 33

Menocal, Francisco, 75–76

menstrual detention, 34, 38–41, 42, 45, 48

menstruation, 23, 24, 37–41. *See also* amenorrhea; menstrual detention

midwifery, 23, 33, 38. *See also* midwives

midwives, 7, 8, 23, 27, 36, 37, 42, 43, 85; as medical experts, 67, 69; performing abortions, 53, 63, 80, 90, 93. *See also* midwifery

mifepristone, 7, 100

miscarriages, 15, 23, 33–34, 40, 53, 59, 69, 75–76, 93; and penal codes, 56, 85. *See also* preterm births

misoprostol, 7, 100

modernization, 12, 51, 119

morality, 15, 19, 21, 24, 47, 71, 74, 87, 89; and doctors, 79, 83, 96, 98, 99, 112, 118; and the law, 106, 108; and public attitudes, 11, 12, 43, 44, 48, 50, 71, 117

mortality, maternal, 2, 53, 65, 85, 86, 96

mortality, neonatal and infant, 33, 44, 63, 72, 86

motherhood, 42, 70, 91; voluntary, 10–11, 101. *See also* maternity

mugwort. See *altamisa*

natality, 51–52, 89, 96, 102

National Academy of Medicine, 97, 99

Navarro y Cardona, Eduardo, 76–77

O'Brien, Elizabeth, 21, 73, 75, 76, 77, 81

obstetrics, 38, 42, 74–80, 93, 96, 98. *See also* gynecology

Ortiz-Ortega, Adriana, 74, 75, 93–94, 101, 103–4

PAN (Partido de Acción Nacional), 5, 92, 111, 112

papacy, 10, 17, 19, 20, 22. *See also* Innocent XI (pope); John Paul II (pope); Pius IX (pope); Pius XI (pope)

Paulina case, 3–4, 111–12, 119

penal code: of 1871, 7, 8, 9, 26, 49, 52–56, 85, 106–7; of 1929, 85; of 1931, 10, 86–87, 97; of Chiapas, 5, 10, 86–87; of Chihuahua, 10, 86–87; of Coahuila, 4; of the Federal District, 1–3, 93–94; of Oaxaca, 56; of Puebla, 56; reforms of, 103–5, 110; of Sonora, 56, 90; of Tlaxcala, 56, 65; of Veracruz, 127n44; of Yucatán, 10, 56, 86–87

pharmacists. See *boticarios*

physicians. *See* doctors

Pius IX (pope), 17, 21, 22

Pius XI (pope), 17, 91

Porfiriato, 9, 51, 55, 66, 70, 72, 81, 107

poverty, 10, 42, 44, 86–87, 96, 98, 105, 108, 118

pre-Columbian medicine, 7–8, 36–37. *See also* Mayan medicine

pregnancy, 3, 4, 6, 7, 23, 24, 36, 41, 45, 46, 53, 78, 126n32. *See also* gestation; quickening

pre-term births, 76–80

PRI (Partido Revolucionario Institucional), 2, 12, 51, 103

To order or obtain more information on these or other University of Nebraska Press titles, visit nebraskapress.unl.edu.

www.ingramcontent.com/pod-product-compliance
Lightning Source LLC
Chambersburg PA
CBHW030848270326
41928CB00008B/1276